The Anglican Church Today:

Catholics in Crisis

FRANCIS PENHALE

MOWBRAY
LONDON & OXFORD

To Chrissie and Sarah with love

First published 1986
by A. R. Mowbray & Co. Ltd,
Saint Thomas House, Becket Street,
Oxford, OX1 1SJ

Typeset by Cotswold Typesetting Ltd, Cheltenham
Printed in Great Britain by Biddles Ltd., Guildford

British Library Cataloguing in Publication Data
Penhale, Francis
The Anglican Church today: Catholics
in crisis. – (Lambeth series)
1. Church of England – Parties and
movements   2. Anglo-Catholicism
I. Title   II. Series
283'.42   BX5121

ISBN 0-264-67083-3

Contents

Preface   *page* vii

Acknowledgements   viii

1 **Introduction**   1

2 **The Catholic Revolution**   5

A short history of the Catholic Movement   5
The revolution by tradition   17
Charisma and clericalism   22
The church within a Church   25

3 **The Meaning of 'Catholicism'**   28

The Tractarians   29
Liberal and radical Catholicism   34
Theory and practice   42

4 **Ritualism and Re-enchantment**   46

Rationalization and re-enchantment   46
A case study: Benediction   50
Explaining ritualism   58
The new disenchantment   63

5 **Parishes and Priests**   69

The priest's role   70
Bishops and priests   72
An ideal type   74
The priest today   78

6 **The Religious Orders** 83

Introduction 83
The beginning of Anglican orders 87
The male orders 93
The religious orders today 99

7 **Walsingham** 102

Introduction 102
The coming of Father Patten 104
The revival of the cult 107
The development of pilgrimage 111
Walsingham since the 1960s 114
The significance of Walsingham 117

8 **Catholic Socialism** 121

Introduction 121
Maurice and Headlam 123
From the Christian Social Union to the
 Catholic Crusade 128
Catholic Socialism today 136

9 **Conclusions** 140

Catholicism and change 140
Priests and professionalism 146
Misogynism and homosexuality 147
The future of Catholicism 149

References 152

Preface

This book is an attempt to understand the present state of the Anglican Catholic movement, in part by a reconsideration of its history. I have drawn on the work of modern historians and sociologists, as well as the literature of the movement in the nineteenth and twentieth centuries and a great number of conversations with Anglican Catholics over the past twenty years. In particular I have used material gained through a survey of pilgrims to Walsingham in 1967-68 and subsequent follow-up correspondence and interviews; in all of this I was greatly helped by the late Canon Colin Stephenson and Mr Stanley Smith. Chapter 4 is a revised version of a paper first published in the *Sociological Yearbook of Religion in Britain*, 4, 1971.

Over the years I have had the benefit of conversation and advice from many people. The few mentioned here, some now dead, must stand proxy for the rest (while of course not being responsible in any way for my opinions): Derek Allen, Stephen Ashton, Jack Boggis, Norman Brown, Wilfred Browning, Christopher Bryant, Robert Carnell, John Crisp, Douglas Fryer, John Gaskell, Phillip Gray, Mike Hawker, Mike Hill, Ken Leech, David Martin, Robin Osborne, Jack Putterill, Kenneth Ross, Bill Sargent, John Vaughan-Jones. I should especially like to thank Richard Holloway for advice on the preparation of the manuscript.

Francis Penhale

ACKNOWLEDGEMENTS

The author and publisher wish to express their thanks to the following for permission to quote material from sources of which they are the publishers or copyright holders. If there are any unwitting breaches of copyright we offer sincere apologies, and will acknowledge them in any future editions.

Basil Blackwell: *The Breaking of the Image* by David Martin.

The Bowerdean Press: *Essays Catholic and Radical,* edited by Kenneth Leech and Rowan Williams.

Croom Helm Ltd: *Class and Religion in the Late Victorian City* by Hugh McLeod.

Darton, Longman and Todd: *Catholic Anglicans Today* edited by John Wilkinson; and *Walsingham Way* and *Merrily on High,* both by Colin Stephenson. *Merrily on High* is published in the United States by Morehouse-Barlow.

J. M. Dent: *Jesus the Heretic* by Conrad Noel.

Gower Publishing Co. Ltd: *Sociology of English Religion* by David Martin, first published by Heinemann Educational Books.

Merlin Press Ltd: *Conrad Noel and the Thaxted Movement* by Reg Groves.

Oxford University Press: *A History of the Church of England 1945-1980* (1984) by Paul A. Welsby.

Penguin Books Ltd: *The Church in the Age of Revolution* by Alec R. Vidler, copyright Alec R. Vidler 1961.

Routledge and Kegan Paul: *The Religious and the Secular* by David Martin.

SCM Press Ltd: *The Church of England 1900-1965* by Roger Lloyd; and *Paths in Spirituality* by John Macquarrie.

SPCK: 'Requiem for Anglican Catholicism?' by Alan Wilkinson, published in *Theology,* January 1978.

Weidenfeld and Nicholson: *The Victorian Debate: English Literature and Society 1832-1901* by Raymond Chapman.

1

Introduction

The flame of truth and justice was kept alive in all ages by heroic souls who were content to be persecuted and scorned as quacks and heretics; sometimes they protested against the accepted theology of their age, sometimes against its political corruptions. These small groups are in every generation the salt of the earth, and without them a living orthodoxy will be stifled by dull conventionality.

Conrad Noel

This book is a study of an enterprise in the renewal of belief. It is concerned with the conflicts which occurred when Victorian Anglicans rediscovered a traditional vision of reality and sought to convey it to others by symbolic means – specifically, the doctrine and ceremonies of Catholic Christianity – and the impact of that vision on the Church of England in the nineteenth and twentieth centuries.

Anglican Catholicism arose early in the industrial age, responding to the stresses and anxieties created by rapid social change. It appealed to those who, in Hugh McLeod's words, 'found liberal Protestantism too insubstantial, and longed for the security offered by tradition and dogma, for the beauty and mystery of Catholic worship'.[1] For while some Victorians sought liberty, others demanded more authority, miracle and magic.

But what was intended by Anglican Catholics to be a means of conveying religious truths became also, and inevitably, politicized – the emblem of party. Deeply-felt and enduring conflicts, expressed in the language of religious symbolism, arose to divide the Victorian Church in ways which to some extent persist to the present day. Both the religious and the political aspects of Catholicism became inseparable components of beliefs strongly held, or rejected, by contending factions within the Church. As one individual caught by the Catholic vision but well aware of its social consequences wrote:

1

'The Mass and the Confessional were bugbears to Protestant England; their reappearance in the National Church was viewed with horror and gave Dissenters further reason for separation from it. They were in fact the two things that I needed. The rather cultured Nonconformity in which I was brought up gave me a picture of Christ as someone long ago who told us the truth about God, bringing home his love and strengthening us by His example, but it was a tale of long ago. I wanted Someone here and now. Catholicism taught the real Presence of Christ among us through the Apostolic Sacraments.'[2] And it was the idea of a God not remote but immediate and sacramentally available which was the most powerful element in Anglican Catholicism. By means of elaborate rites, often performed in purpose-built neo-Gothic churches, Catholics provided forms of religious experience which to many Victorians and their successors were dramatic and compelling.

Anglo-Catholicism in fact appealed at a number of levels, as McLeod makes clear. One of these was the quest for the certainty given by an unshakeable authority. 'This searching for authority at a time when old authorities were collapsing was certainly one reason for the attractiveness of Anglo-Catholicism in the late nineteenth century, and familiar to those who have tried to explain conversions of intellectuals to the Roman Catholic Church in the twentieth century. But this is not enough to explain the range of the Catholic appeal: an appeal to ultra-democrats as much as to ultra-conservatives, to the theologically liberal as much as to the authoritarian. Catholicism answered to a need of beauty and a need for community, felt to be lacking in Protestantism. It also appealed to those who longed for a sense of "the Church" and its true grandeur, and those who wanted a religion freed from the respectability and the puritanism of the churches in which they had grown up.'[3]

Many of these things were not apparent at the beginning of the movement; McLeod is speaking of a time fifty or more years later. At first Anglican Catholicism seemed essentially conservative, even reactionary, and thus had strong similarities to what Peter Berger has called the 'de-modernizing impulse', which opposes and attempts to alter the technological and bureaucratic forces at work in contemporary society. In both cases there is a rejection of current directions of change, and a desire either to maintain the status quo or to return to an earlier and better way of life.

The extent to which this is actually possible is often severely limited. As Berger concludes, de-modernization, at least in its more radical manifestations, has definite limits,[4] and this seems true also of Anglican Catholicism, which flourished for more than a century but now appears to be in a state of gradual decline, despite recent campaigns for 'Catholic renewal'. But appearances may be deceptive: the survival of the movement for over one hundred and fifty years suggests some inherent resilience, even if at present few positive signs are visible. Congregations and religious orders both age and decline, with few exceptions, as part of the general marginalization of Christianity in British culture; doctrinal orthodoxy corrodes under the acids of liberalism; and where Catholic traditions persist, they are sometimes more the pietism of the altar boy, or a well-intentioned if narrow search for communality and relevance, than the balanced diet of orthodoxy.

Probably in the short run the pattern will be unaltered. This does not mean either that the movement will eventually collapse altogether or that it is incapable of revival, though there are those in its ranks today who embrace both views, often with a curious religious masochism. In any case, both for those who are committed and for those who are merely interested, an investigation of the past can provide an understanding on which attempts to anticipate the future may be based.

The terminology employed requires a word of explanation. Members of the Catholic movement in the Church of England have been variously known as Tractarians, Puseyites, Ritualists, Anglo-Catholics and High Church. Each of these terms has a distinct and specific historical reference, though some of them have been used synonymously from time to time. For the sake of consistency and simplicity in this book I shall employ 'Catholics' and 'Catholicism' as generic terms to refer to Anglicans belonging to these groups. Roman Catholics will be referred to as such.[5]

The plan of the book is as follows. First I outline the history of the movement and consider some of its features in the light of studies carried out from a sociological perspective. Then in successive chapters I discuss the beliefs of Anglican Catholics, the significance of ritualism, the priest's role, the religious orders, the development of the Walsingham shrine and some political features of the movement. No claim to comprehensiveness is made. I see the book as a series of essays by means of which aspects of the movement can be approached, while acknowledging that much has been omitted or dealt with cursorily.

Some of my comments are critical, especially in the final chapter. This does not mean that I am yet another sociological 'cultured despiser' of religion (an image which anyway deserves decent interment by now). On the contrary, such religion as I have is a product of Anglican Catholicism. And it is my understanding of what the Catholic movement once was, and could be again, which leads me to criticize some of its present features.

2

The Catholic Revolution

When the potentials damned up in the Church and the
sect slowly begin to brim over the edge, a dynamic is set
in motion. . . . It begins, usually, in an attempt to tighten
up the observance of God's law and to make his word
come with power. The dull images start to shine, the
somnolent rituals are shaken alive. Men strive to be
perfect, even as their Father in heaven is perfect.

David Martin

A revolution is literally a 'turning-over', an overturning, of
existing arrangements. Originally used in a political sense, it
has become broadened in the course of time to cover any form
of change, social or intellectual, of a particularly far-reaching
kind. Moreover, it need not be understood as necessarily
involving innovation: the recovery of forgotten traditional
insights can be equally radical in its effects.

It is in this sense that we can talk of a 'Catholic revolution'.
Anglo-Catholics saw the Church of England at the beginning of
the nineteenth century as a corrupt institution in a state of
major decline. To be saved and renewed, they argued, it must
recover an understanding of its true nature as a part of the one
catholic and apostolic Church which Christ had founded. The
exploration of this foundational principle in both theory and
practice, in theology, worship, spirituality and institutional
forms, was to overturn the Anglicanism of the early 1800s, and
to put something very different in its place.

A short history of the Catholic movement

In the course of its development Anglican Catholicism has
experienced a number of major transitions. Four roughly-
defined stages may be distinguished: the Oxford Movement
(1833-45); the rise of ritualism (1845-1920); the Congress
period (1920-48); and the age of uncertainty (1948 to date).

5

The Oxford Movement

The beginning of the Oxford Movement is conventionally
dated, following Newman, from the Assize Sermon preached
by John Keble in the university church of St Mary in Oxford on
the fourteenth of July 1833 with the theme of 'National
Apostasy'. In this he strongly criticized the government
proposal to suppress ten Irish bishoprics. The Irish proposals
were the (relatively modest) parliamentary response to an anti-
church and anti-clerical movement which had flourished
throughout the 1820s, bringing together Dissenters, radicals,
tithe-payers and others in a demand for reform which the
Church had been unwilling or unable to meet. While this was
the immediate issue, more fundamentally the Oxford Movement was also, as Kenneth Thompson has argued, a reaction to
the pressures generated by an increasingly complex and
pluralistic society which were increasingly relegating the
Church to a subordinate position in British society at the
beginning of the nineteenth century.[1] Religious and political
issues were intertwined with wider patterns of social change.

There were also grievances of a different sort, at the blatant
erastianism of a Church which appeared to be little more than
an arm of the state. To this the Tractarians opposed the vision
of an autonomous Church, conscious of its essentially supernatural character, concerned with spiritual goals, and
grounded in a more sacerdotal conception of ministry. As
Anthony Russell observes, this new understanding of the role
of the clergyman, centred on his function as celebrant of the
sacraments, would clearly be attractive to a newly self-
conscious group in search of legitimacy.[2]

In addition, alarm was felt in church circles on a number of
other issues: the growth of theological liberalism; the threat
which the Roman Catholic Church appeared to present to
Anglicanism following the passing of the Catholic Emancipa-
tion Act of 1829; and the general enfeeblement of church life
at the time. More positively, there was growing interest in the
cultural forms of the early and medieval Church, inspired by
the Romantic movement. Medievalism offered, as Alice
Chandler has suggested in her study of the medieval ideal in
nineteenth century English literature, a 'dream of order': a
half-mythical, half-historical vision of a more humane and
stable way of life which was supposed to have prevailed in the
Middle Ages. It was part of a quest for beauty and meaning in
an age becoming increasingly depersonalized and industrial-
ized. Neither modern science nor contemporary social

developments gave man any grounds for believing that he was at home in the universe. Medievalism was one of the last great religious expressions of the human need to belong.[3] But, according to Alice Chandler, it was bound to fail, since the belief that the universe is made for man has no basis in logic.[4] The Tractarians and their successors would, of course, disagree.

The response to such factors, which led eventually to a full-blown Anglican Catholic movement, was developed at first by a coterie of close acquaintances centred around J. H. Newman at Oriel College Oxford, including Keble, E. B. Pusey, R. W. Church, R. H. Froude, C. Marriott, R. I. Wilberforce and I. Williams. Following Keble's sermon there was a house party at Hadleigh, in Suffolk to consider what to do next. No agreement could be reached on this, but as a consequence a society was set up which sent a memorial with the names and signatures of 6,530 clergy to the Archbishop of Canterbury, while at a later stage 230,000 heads of families supported the apostolic form of church government. While these signatures were being collected, the *Tracts for the Times*, which were to give the movement its early name, were begun by Newman. Between 1833 and 1841, ninety tracts were issued. They argued that the Church of England should recover a sense of the unchangeability of Catholic truth, the divine and holy nature of the Church, and its spiritual authority. From the last followed the stress on the apostolic succession of the ministry. As *Tract One* said, 'On what are the clergy to rest their authority when the State deserts them? Upon nothing else than their Apostolic descent.'[5] This claim can be seen as a direct response to the threat perceived in theological liberalism, and to problems of church-state relations. The Tractarians argued that the Church was not a creation of the state; its commission began in apostolic times and the line of continuity had never been broken.

At first there was a good deal of support for Tractarian views, though they were opposed by liberals; but as the Tractarian ideology developed, problems arose concerning the location of the Catholicism which it proclaimed. Was this truly to be found in Canterbury–or in Rome? A pronounced Romanizing theme became apparent in the movement, provoking alarm and hostility among the Evangelical and traditional high church elements. Matters came to a head in 1845, when Ward, Faber and Newman were received into the Church of Rome. However, a majority of the group remained in the Church of

England, and continued to develop under the leadership of Pusey.

The rise of ritualism

The Tractarian movement was largely academic in membership and centred on Oxford. After 1845, however, it spread out into the parishes and attracted a much wider basis of support. 'The Tracts were converted into acts.'[6] There now developed the interest in liturgy, ceremonial, architecture and music which had already been present at the earlier stage. Church architecture became focused around the requirements of ritual, and was employed to illustrate eucharistic principles through elaborate altars, ornate rood screens and long chancels. Much of this was based on the liturgical studies carried out in Cambridge by the Camden (later the Ecclesiological) Society, founded in 1839 by E. J. Boyce, J. M. Neale and Benjamin Webb. Within four years this society had seven hundred ordinary members as well as two archbishops, sixteen bishops, twenty-one archdeacons and rural deans, sixteen architects and thirty-one peers and MPs. It published *The Ecclesiologist* and many other works in which its principles were set out, notably the *Hierurgia Anglicana* (1843-8). Its initial reference point was Anglican custom of the seventeenth century, and it took the trouble to assure the anxious that what was done was entirely compatible with post-Reformation rite and usage. Charles Lloyd and William Palmer, representatives of the old high church school, revived Prayer Book studies in the eighteen-thirties and prepared the ground for ritualism by discussion of seventeenth century custom and practice, and of what was allowed by the Ornaments Rubric. However, they also began the introduction of much more far-reaching considerations, by their discussion of the extent to which the Prayer Book was related to the customs of the ancient Church of the first centuries.

While the initial reference point was the seventeenth century, changes could be justified in terms of what was legally permissible. There was also a pragmatic element, since pictorial examples from that period were used as a source of ideas for altar furnishings and vestments. But recognition that much Prayer Book material came from earlier periods, and growing knowledge of the ceremonial which had accompanied it, gradually undermined the exclusiveness of reference. The Tractarians began to think about what had been lost at the Reformation, to go beyond merely citing Anglican formularies,

and to widen the scope of desirable usage. In short, they
began to look at what had been done by the early Church, and
to relate this to the claim of apostolic succession. If the
Church of England was indeed truly within that line of descent
it was entitled to employ rites and ceremonies which the early
Church had used, and which, Tractarians came to feel, were
being unjustifiably neglected. Once this position had been
adopted, a further step was to see the Roman Catholic Church
as a legitimate source; Rome had 'a ritual, which ... sets
before the eyes more prominently than our own, our Saviour
in His Life and Death for His Church', as Pusey wrote in 1842.
And once Rome was seen in this light, the whole range of
Roman sacramentalism was theoretically accessible.

Not all of this was apparent at the beginning. The immediate
concern of parish clergy influenced by Tractarianism was to
introduce regular and reverent worship, and later to make the
Holy Communion the central act of devotion. But the gradual
adoption of a comprehensively sacramental system of thought
involved the doctrine that Christ is present in some sense in
the bread and wine of the Eucharist. Tractarian thought
evolved from the belief in a presence which was real but
spiritual, to the position taken in the eighteen-fifties by Keble,
Pusey and Wilberforce that the presence was *objectively* real,
and that this should be made apparent by elaborate dress and
ceremony. But ritualism is not to be explained solely by
doctrinal development. The complex range of factors which
brought about the full-blooded ritualism practised at the turn
of the century are discussed further in Chapter 4.

Usually the Holy Communion as first celebrated by Tractarian clergy would be an early service preceded by fasting,
(since this was thought more convenient for servants and
labourers). Afternoon and evening Communions were considered by Catholics to be against the teaching and practice of
the early Church, and also undesirable since they discouraged
fasting. Pusey wrote to T. T. Carter in 1844 suggesting that he
should have weekly Communions at an early hour. Samuel
Wilberforce had three celebrations a month at Alverstoke;
Butler of Wantage maintained a traditional pattern of monthly
communion initially, but prefaced this by very extensive
preparation, with twelve classes of different types of parishioners in the week preceding. Robert Suckling saw it as his
duty 'to offer the sacrifice every Sunday'. By the early 1860s,
monthly Communion was the norm, weekly services were
found in a number of parishes, and there were a few instances

of a daily celebration, e.g. at St Peter's, London Docks, St Peter's Plymouth and St Saviour's, Leeds. But, as Anthony Russell observes, this was exceptional, and even a weekly Communion was so unusual as to be a public demonstration of Tractarian sympathies.[7]

There was an increase in other forms of daily service, largely confined to those influenced by Tractarian views. Keble began daily morning prayer at Otterbourne in 1838, Wilberforce had daily prayers at Alverstock from 1841 onwards, Butler began daily service at Wantage in 1846, and Bennett at St Barnabas, Pimlico from 1847. A number of other examples could be quoted, but in the 1850s the daily service, though more common, was still an exception to the rule.

Initially only simple ornaments (a plain cross, candlesticks etc.) were employed. At first progress beyond this was slow: by 1850 there were only two places in England where the eucharistic vestments were worn, and they were not found in London until 1859. In the same year incense was first used at a Christmas midnight Communion service at St Mary Magdalene's, Munster Square.[8] Yet despite this, the fears of some church leaders were stated early on, and in very forceful terms. An attack on the movement by Bishop Blomfield of London in 1842 gives a clear indication of the anxiety felt in the highest quarters about where it all might lead. And the bishop was remarkably prescient, fulminating against those who 'evidence a desire and longing to revert, not merely to some of the outward ceremonies, but to the devotional formularies of the Church of Rome; that they should speak disparagingly and disrespectfully of our Liturgy, and prepare men of ardent feelings and warm imaginations for a return to the Romish mass book, by publishing for daily use devotions and homilies taken from authors of that Church, and embodying not a few of its superstitions and unscriptural doctrines and practices; that they should recommend, or justify, under any qualification, prayers or addresses to saints, which began in poetry and ended in idolatry; intercessions for the dead, which our Church, by her formal discontinuance of them, has implicitly forbidden, and which tend directly to the notion of purgatory; and auricular confession, a practice utterly unknown to the Primitive Church, one of the most fearful abuses of that of Rome, and the source of unspeakable abominations'.[9]

Blomfield thus saw ceremonial as closely tied to doctrine. The Tractarians would have agreed with this while rejecting his interpretation of their aims. Pusey, in 1849, was anxious to set the emerging ritual conflicts in a proper context. The development of proper ceremony was not a matter of mere taste for ritual *per se*. It was a means to an end. 'I think it is of great moment that we should not foster the impression that this great battle is about things external ... (once the content of our teaching has been grasped) there will be no more battles about surplices. There will be a deeper strife, but it will be with the world.'[10]

This deeper strife was not immediately evident. Instead, the following century was marked by a series of conflicts with both ecclesiastical authorities and laity which may seem bizarre and trivial from the perspective of the 1980s. 'Advanced' ceremonial and ornament became more common, involving the vestments worn by the priest, the ritual actions which he performed, portable lights, incense, and the use of men and boys as servers. There were two sources for such innovations. One was the Ornaments Rubric of the 1549 Prayer Book, which, it was claimed, legally required them. Sometimes the form in which they were employed was patterned on the so-called 'Sarum use' found at Salisbury Cathedral in the Middle Ages. The second source for change was current Roman Catholic practice, thus giving further support to the widespread fear of 'popery'.

Conflict developed over the legitimacy of ritual and the doctrine which it expressed. Archdeacon Denison was prosecuted before the Archbishop of Canterbury's Commission in the years 1854-56 for teaching the doctrine of the real presence of Christ in the consecrated sacrament in two sermons given in Wells Cathedral. Moderate sections of both clergy and laity felt alarm at the threat to church order, as they understood it, which was presented by ritualism. After the passing of the Public Worship Act of 1874, a special court was set up under Lord Penzance to try cases dealing with ceremonial and the use of vestments. A number of Catholic clergy were summoned before this court as a result of the activities of the Protestant Church Association, formed in 1865 'to counteract Popery and Ritualism'. In fact no priests ever appeared before the court but *in absentia* five were found guilty and imprisoned in the years 1877-87, for an average of 147 days each.

More spectacular than legal action was the mob violence employed against a number of ritualistic clergy. Militant Protestants harassed ritualistic churches and clergy, bringing about recurrent rioting. In 1851, the church of St Barnabas,

Pimlico was 'veritably a beleaguered city, held by armed men,
against enemies who tried to break down the doors during
divine service, and yelled through the windows, or, gaining
entrance, hooted and hissed in the nave and essayed to
storm the chancel'.[11] At St George's-in-the-East towards the end
of the 1850s, services were disrupted for a year by rioting
Sunday after Sunday, which the police did little to prevent. In
the 1860s the incidence of ritualistic rioting was even greater.

The activities of the early religious orders also attracted
hostility. Priscilla Lydia Sellon, founder of the Devonport Sisterhood, was the subject of extensive malicious gossip and
rumour, leading to a public enquiry in 1849 at which she was
exonerated. In 1857, members of the Community of St
Margaret, East Grinstead, were attacked and stoned while
attending the funeral of a sister. The social concern which was
very much a part of the movement was apparent in the foundation of sisterhoods, and also in the work of slum priests in the
many new urban ritualist churches established from the 1850s
onwards. A belief grew up in some quarters that the priest
should be outside the social hierarchy, no longer an instrument of class-based social control, and that his duty was to all
men regardless of their position or status. How far this ideal
was realized, given the overwhelmingly middle class origins of
the clergy, is questionable. Social issues were tackled in a more
theoretical manner by a number of 'Christian socialist' organi-
zations and individuals, inspired by the writings of F. D.
Maurice, Charles Gore, Stewart Headlam and others, and
leading to the foundation of groups such as the Christian
Social Union and the Church Socialist League.

Controversy was also caused by the development of sacramental confession. This was reintroduced on an individual
basis in the 1840s, when Keble and Pusey acted as confessors
to a small number of people. In the 1850s handbooks for
clergy began to recommend the establishment of a personal
relationship between clergy and parishioners involving
spiritual counselling, but the institution of systematic sacramental confession was not advocated in such texts. When it
began to appear in some parishes it caused much contention,
especially in the furore which occurred in the late 1870s over
the confessors' manual, *The Priest in Absolution*, published by
the Society of the Holy Cross. Catholics claimed that sacramental confession was a legitimate part of the spiritual life of
the Church, and that it helped priests to know their people
better. Opponents argued that a parson should know his

people without such methods, and suspected a prurient interest which led to young ladies being asked improper questions. The scandal caused led to widespread criticism and to a decline in the membership of the Society, but in the course of time the numbers of Anglican penitents grew, though not all Catholics came to make their confession and it remained a minority practice within Anglicanism.

From a sociological viewpoint, a number of reasons for the development of confession may be suggested. Firstly it could, if effective, be a useful means of internalized social control. Secondly, it contributed to a professionalizing strategy, as Anthony Russell notes, enabling the building up of the trust thought typical of professional relationships. Thirdly it might be a necessary device for the urban priest, whose relation to his congregation was more problematic than that of his rural counterpart; his approach had to be individualistic since his status in the community was no longer given.

Throughout the latter part of the nineteenth century and after, the ritualistic controversies were given much public attention. They were debated in Parliament, legislation was passed in an attempt to suppress such practices, and the leading figures were pilloried in *Punch*. Even the episcopate were not immune from ritualist influence or legal sanction: in 1888, Bishop King of Lincoln appeared before the Archbishop of Canterbury, charged with ritual offences. Parliamentary concern and action were recurrent throughout the period and were expressed in the Ritual Commission of 1867, the Royal Commission on Ecclesiastical Discipline of 1904, and the Prayer Book debates of the 1920s.

Yet it was plain that the Catholics had gained much ground. As Roger Lloyd remarks, 'By the end of the nineteenth century the Anglo-Catholics had won, and it was evident that they had won ... they had out-thought, out-lived and out-suffered all their opponents.'[12] One indication of their success is that, according to Kelway, by 1914, vestments were worn in over 5,000 churches.[13]

The early part of the twentieth century was marked by conflicts over the use of incense, the reservation of the consecrated sacrament, devotion to the sacrament in the illegal service of Benediction borrowed from Rome, and the cult of Mary which developed through the establishment of Marian shrines, most notably at Walsingham. But it proved impossible to achieve any effective regulation of public worship, and though clashes over ritualism occurred from time to time, the eventual outcome has been that the limits of the permissible are largely determined informally within parishes.

The Congress Period

The Catholic movement was at its height in the 1920s and 1930s. Many of the earlier conflicts had been resolved legally or otherwise, some Catholic practices having been officially accepted, while others continued though still prohibited. Catholics were ceasing to regard themselves as an embattled minority, and had become aware that their numbers were now very considerable. The Anglo-Catholic Congresses held from 1920 onwards were intended as a public demonstration of this, and also as a means of evangelization. In 1920, the Albert Hall was filled twice daily for a week, and 1,200 priests walked in procession through the streets to St Alban's, Holborn for High Mass. In 1923, 16,000 Anglo-Catholics heard the Bishop of Zanzibar, Frank Weston, preach a passionate call for the conversion of England, received with enormous enthusiasm. In 1933 at the Congress marking the centenary of the movement, 50,000 people attended a pontifical High Mass at the White City, probably the largest Anglican congregation which has ever assembled for worship.[14]

But even in this triumph there was an element of insecurity. The controversy over the 1928 Prayer Book had revealed that the Catholic party was not yet strong enough to dominate the Church of England, and the 1933 Congress report speaks of an outlook 'dark, though not hopeless'.[15] Beyond the walls of Anglican Catholicism, secularism was advancing, and the speakers at the Congress were conscious of this. Moreover the conflicts continued in some areas: an 'advanced' priest, Bernard Walke, Vicar of St Hilary in Cornwall, had been held prisoner by Protestant demonstrators while the ornaments of the church at which he had spent twenty years were smashed before his eyes. One of the most advanced manifestations of Anglican Catholicism, the Shrine of Our Lady of Walsingham in Norfolk was the subject of critical comment even from Catholic journals such as the *Church Times*, reflecting a continuing uncertainty as to what the notion of 'Catholicism' might legitimately embrace. Within the Catholic movement, itself a party within a denomination, there were internal sub-divisions, evidence of both inherent weakness and the loosely defined ideology which held the movement together. Again the fundamental question arose: what after all was the meaning of Catholicism and what norms did it imply?

A further development which, while ostensibly advancing the Catholic cause, was in practice to dilute it still further, was what came to be known as the Parish Communion movement, after the book of that title by Father A. G. Hebert and others published in 1937. Hebert set forth a conception of the Church as separate from the secularized world in which it existed, and of the Eucharist as the meeting of church members at which the parish family expresses its fellowship. ('Family' was to be a greatly overworked term in twentieth century Anglican writings.) The liturgy which developed from the Parish Communion movement possessed some of the externals of Catholic worship – lights, vestments, acolytes – but no necessary Catholic doctrinal content. It was thus open to use either by Catholics treating it as a means of advance to Catholic goals, or by those who thought little of Catholicism but found the idea of a restrained ritual attractive and evangelically useful for their own beliefs (which might well be liberal). I comment further in Chapter 4.

After 1945 the tensions at the extreme end of Anglo-Catholicism became increasingly apparent. The proposals for the creation of the Church of South India generated much conflict and opposition, leading to the emergence of bodies such as the Annunciation Group, which held that the catholic basis of the ministry would be destroyed by introduction into the Church of England of clergy who had not been episcopally ordained. Some clergy became Roman Catholics;[16] but these were few in number, and though the Annunciation Group continued until 1969, its influence was negligible. There are obvious parallels with current debates over the ordination of women.

By 1948, there were further signs of change. For one thing, the movement was becoming more respectable: seventeen bishops attended the Congress in that year. For another, future changes were presaged in the statement that evening Masses and a modification of the fast before Communion were on the way, a statement greeted with cries of horror and protest according to one participant. Thirdly there was a feeling that the triumphalism of the thirties was past, and the movement was entering a different stage, with new insecurities and problems.

The Age of Uncertainty

An important cause of change was the second Vatican Council of the early 1960s. The Roman Catholic Church, a major source of legitimation for Anglo-Catholic practices, began far-reaching changes which effectively undercut many accepted conventions. Liturgical reform and extensive normative revisions were set in motion. The impact on Anglicans was apparent at the Church Union congress of 1968, which was widely interpreted as effectively displaying the changed emphases of the movement. The opening Mass was marked by extreme simplicity, a reflection of the changes in liturgical thinking in the post-war period which were to proceed further in the next decade. The respectability of the movement was apparent in the presence of both Princess Margaret and the Archbishop of Canterbury. And finally, acknowledging the advance of secularization in the post-war period, the organizing secretary of the Church Union spoke of 'the lapse of the majority of our nation into unbelief or indifference' and the problems which make 'it hard for the average Catholic to persevere with his faith'.

Anglican Catholicism, like the wider Church, had now entered into a period of considerable uncertainty. Many of the goals for which its forefathers had fought had been achieved: Catholic teaching, liturgical reform, the development of religious orders, and a more spiritual conception of the Church. But as the organizing secretary also remarked, Catholics were beset by 'the swamping demands of everyday life' and 'new ideas about faith, discipline, morals and worship'. New forms were being sought as a response to growing secularity, while numbers fell and causes passionately advocated thirty years before were now disregarded. Modern liberal theology had found a home in some quarters of the Catholic movement itself, and the Parish Communion movement, based in part on Anglo-Catholic foundations had brought about what some saw as a sentimental cult of the family and a dilution of Catholic teaching. From the 1960s onwards, much liturgical revision took place within the Church of England, as elsewhere. It has had the unintended consequence of promoting more diversity, conflict over the loss of the traditional Prayer Book services valued by many, and a certain liturgical insecurity within congregations as customary practice becomes more varied. As the *General Instruction on the Liturgy* observes, 'common bodily attitudes are a sign of the community and unity of the assembly'; the symbolic implications for a church in which the opposite is found need hardly be spelt out, and members of congregations are often well aware of this.

In the late 1970s, the Church Union led a movement for Catholic Renewal. Acknowledging a loss of nerve in the 1960s its leaders sought to regain ground, and a new form of conference, smaller in numbers and seeking a major reconsideration of the nature and purpose of Anglican Catholicism, was held at Loughborough. It was also at this time that an Anglican Catholic left re-emerged under the title of the Jubilee Group. Members of this group condemned the Catholic movement for its loss of social concern and a preoccupation with 'lace, gin and backbiting', and saw a trend towards 'a sickly pietism and a right-wing reactionary stance in social and political issues' which they found very disturbing.

In 1983, one hundred and fifty years of Anglican Catholicism was celebrated with an open air Mass in the University Parks in Oxford and many other events. At this time no significant changes in the recent fortunes of the movement were apparent. While retaining considerable numerical strength, it did not appear to have recovered any strong sense of direction, and was facing a problem of ageing, painfully apparent in some congregations, as many members of the younger generation with a religious interest turned either to the exotic 'new religions' or to a revived and dynamic Evangelicalism.

By the middle of the 1980s, signs of a major loss of confidence were apparent. The movement for Catholic Renewal had only limited impact, and a second Loughborough conference was widely said to be a failure. The ordination of women became a central issue, and although bodies such as the Church Union made a firm stand against this, there were divisions within the ranks of Catholics. Some of the women who went abroad to be ordained came from the Catholic wing of the Church, and were supported by fellow Catholics in favour of female priests. Thus at one extreme there was a refusal to toe the party line. But at the other extreme some Catholics, appalled at the damage they feared Anglican unilateralism might inflict on Catholic order, left the Church of England for Roman or Orthodox alternatives. The familiar divisions remained.

The revolution by tradition

In part, Catholicism can be characterized as a movement of critical negation, in opposition to many worldly beliefs and practices. This is not because 'the world' as such is condemned – on the contrary it is made sacred and holy by the incarnational event, the coming of Christ, and by the continued divine action within it. Catholicism affirms the worth both of the material world and of human nature. What it rejects is any misuse of either, any distortion of man or world from their divinely ordained form. Such distortions are of course possible and often found, given free will and the defects of human nature. One function of the Catholic Church therefore is to recall both individuals and institutions to the way of Christ.

It does so on the basis of traditional authority. This might seem to make it conservative, even reactionary at times, and certainly the desire to conserve that which has been shown to be of value is a powerful element in the Catholic economy. But while Catholic Christianity often appears *merely* conservative in a pejorative sense, it possesses a latent critical force, firmly rooted in orthodoxy, which can promote a subversion of existing ways.

Human groups—institutions, communities, even whole societies—possess at least a minimal degree of consensus, shared beliefs and ways of doing things. In other words, they have standards. The degree to which these standards are observed inevitably varies in the course of time. Whenever departures from such standards take place the authority of tradition can be employed as a basis for recalling the group to the original pristine intention. This may appear to be innovation, especially to those who have not retained the tradition, but as Littledale says, 'Remember what Innovation means. It is the introduction of a new thing, unknown before. If something which is old, and has been worn out by use, or has been stolen, is replaced, we do not call that replacement Innovation, but Restoration.' [17]

However, the relationship between communities, individuals and rules is rather more complicated than this, as Michael Hill[18] makes clear in his discussion of the ideal type of traditional authority developed by the sociologist Max Weber.[19] He distinguishes the *normative* element, defined as the 'sanctity of immemorial traditions', from the *social* element, the individuals who exercise authority under the constraints of tradition. Weber appears to attach far more importance to the latter, and stresses that in practice obedience is owed, not to the tradition as such, but to the person who occupies a position founded on traditional authority.

Traditional authority is therefore to some extent flexible. Traditional leaders and institutions have considerable autonomy within a broadly defined area in which they can always claim as traditional what is in fact new, by arguing that it has always existed although only recently recognized. Against this, the traditions themselves determine the content of commands and the extent of authority, and thus provide a check on the individual leader. He can be resisted because he has not observed the traditional limits of his authority. The normative component of legitimate authority can thus form the basis for what in a particular context may appear to be revolutionary change, although it is really, in Littledale's term, restoration. This is a 'revolution by tradition': change justified by reference to an authority based on precedent.[20]

The exercise of traditional authority can be complicated by the plurality of traditions which may exist at any given time: there is no reason to assume a single unitary tradition. Where a tradition is pluralistic, there are three possibilities: (i) an attempt to make one version of 'the tradition' universal; (ii) a struggle for dominance between advocates of different versions within a continuing pluralism; or (iii) a 'bargaining' situation: negotiation between contending groups which may lead to an acceptable compromise and fusion of versions. Christianity has known all three of these possibilities.

The Church of England is often described as both 'Catholic and Reformed'. It is inherently pluralistic. There are various 'parties' within the Church, and, in the nineteenth century especially, they adhered to separate accounts of the source of the traditional authority used to support their claims.[21] Different historical periods were regarded as defining that version of the 'true nature' of the Church which they wished to advance. Protestants saw a fundamental break as occurring at the Reformation, by which the purity of the early Church was restored after the corruption and abuses of medieval Catholicism. The Church of England was thought to be unquestionably Protestant, and to have more in common with Protestant Churches elsewhere than with Rome. On the other hand Catholics asserted a progressive cumulation of tradition from the beginning; there have been periods of growth and periods of decline, but the continuity from the earliest days is unbroken. The Middle Ages may have had undesirable features (though even this would sometimes be denied), but fundamentally was the high point of catholicity, and medieval society was seen as containing communitarian elements which had been lost since and to which a return was sought. The use of the term *Ecclesia Anglicana* in nineteenth century literature frequently indicated this kind of viewpoint.

The high value attached to medieval Catholicism in the

nineteenth century arose in part from the Romantic movement and from antiquarian research especially into church architecture by groups like the Camden Society, and encouraged a view of the medieval period as a 'golden age' from which there had been a subsequent decline. This view had its counterpart on the continent in the Romantic reaction to the excesses of the French Revolution, where a similar high view of past society, and especially of religion, was to be found. The positive attitude to medievalism was the opposite of its denigration during the eighteenth century, when the 'age of reason' even led to the rejection of Gothic architecture as aesthetically imperfect, and to the whitewashing of church interiors to symbolize 'the illumination of religion by the pure light of reason'.[22] But a strong anti-catholic tradition remained, and this was one of the forces with which nineteenth century Anglican Catholics had to cope.

Two other historical reference points were employed. The first was the Church of the New Testament period as described in the scriptures. This was sharply defined to exclude the early Fathers. The second was a broader category, 'the early Church', including not only the New Testament period but also the first five centuries, down to the Council of Chalcedon in 451. It was this which formed the basis for the Tractarians' revolution by tradition. A central principle of the Oxford Movement was that 'the early Church' should be the model for the reform of the Church of England, a view which had previously been held by the high church tradition of the sixteenth and seventeenth centuries, especially the Nonjurors. But it had become obscured, even rejected, by the rationalistic and erastian Church of the eighteenth century; the Tractarians sought to recall the earlier view and its significance.

This was something which they had in common with Wesley, though they were to put it to rather different use. Wesley had employed 'the early Church' to legitimate his own reforms, and had even gone through a shortlived 'high church' phase; he was a patristic student and some of the practices which he introduced into Methodism were, or were claimed to be, revivals of primitive church customs. Methodism followed a different course later, according to Hill, for two reasons; firstly because of the selective use of traditional standards made by the typical local leaders of Methodism at the end of the eighteenth century – small manufacturers and traders who favoured inner worldly asceticism because of the benefits it gave them in the form of industrial work discipline; and,

secondly, because Wesley himself tended to stress an innova-
tory image of the early Church to justify his own policies. In
contrast, it can be suggested that the Catholic leadership was
deeply immersed in the conservative, academic and rural
values of the established middle classes, and was therefore pre-
disposed to accept the full range of traditional elements if an
adequate basis of legitimacy could be provided.

Wesleyanism had much in common with Evangelicalism,
especially a strongly emotional approach. Evangelicals played
down intellectual activity such as patristic scholarship in
favour of biblical literalism, and they looked to the Reformation for a model. There is also a link between Evangelicalism
and Tractarianism; this lies in the attempt at revitalization of
Christianity, and the longing for a living knowledge and love of
God, as Allchin suggests.[23] A number of Tractarians, including
Newman, had an Evangelical upbringing, and this no doubt
explains the dual element in their thought – a stress on
experience as well as tradition. The Evangelical/Catholic link
is found later, for example in Father Benson of Cowley, and is
a distinctive feature of the Anglo-Catholic movement, not
always noted.

To use the early Church as an *exclusive* model, as Pusey did,
presented certain difficulties, the most obvious of which was
its remoteness in time, and hence a dependence on the interpretations of scholars. Also, for anyone attached to a continuity
theory, such an approach raises the question of what had
occurred historically between the early Church and Anglicanism. The obvious answer is the Roman Catholic Church, which
still exists as a continuing source of authority. Considerations
of this sort gave the Puseyan approach a certain historical
mustiness by comparison with the living authority of Rome,
which moreover denied the validity of the Tractarian claims.
Rome could be interpreted in a 'Protestant' way as corrupt and
needing reform at the time of the Reformation, but it existed
as a living denial of what the Tractarians claimed about the
Church of England, and its vitality after the Catholic Emancipa-
tion Act of 1829 was to prove a magnet to uncertain Anglican
Catholics from the time of Newman onwards: 'poping' was,
and remains, always an option for the doubter. A 'Protestant'
response was again possible: to assert that while Anglicans saw
tradition as only confirming the truth of scripture, Romans
saw it as supplementary, thus implying the inadequacy of
scripture alone and opening the way to the legitimation of
superstitious accretions of doctrine and practice.

The Oxford Movement sought both to preserve and to reform within the Church of their day. The apostolic succession in the Anglican episcopate, then under threat from low church and political sources, was to be defended; but they also wanted changes in religious organization which involved reinstatement of early church practices, for example, frequent communion with preparation including fasting, and daily services. Particularly they wished to assert the spiritual autonomy of the Church in an erastian age, its status as a 'perfect society', and to employ the early Church, which they saw as clearly separate from the state, as a model for achieving this within the Church of England. In part they would do so by employing another mode of authority distinguished by Weber, the charismatic type. To emphasize the charismatic element of an office, whether bishop or priest, is one way of asserting spiritual authority, one of the signs of the perfect society. This is discussed next.

Charisma and clericalism

The term 'charisma' is of course one of the most abused in sociology, having entered everyday speech as a way of referring to anyone considered 'striking' or 'impressive'. Weber defines it more rigorously as 'a certain quality of an individual personality by virtue of which' a person 'is set apart from ordinary men and treated as endowed with supernatural, superhuman, or at least specifically exceptional powers or qualities. These are such as are not accessible to the ordinary person, but are regarded as of divine origin or as exemplary, and on the basis of them the individual concerned is treated as a leader'.[24] There is still a certain vagueness in this definition, since Weber appears to understand the attribution of such powers as either supernatural or natural, and as covering a range from the divinely inspired 'berserker' to the demagogic intellectual, but it will suffice for considering the role of personalities within Anglo-Catholicism.

From the beginning of the movement there has been a tendency to hagiography. Leaders from the Oxford period onwards have been singled out and discussed in terms of the special qualities which gave them a following. Newman, for example, inspired a clique of ardent young men, later to become the basis of his community at Littlemore, to regard him as a singularly spiritual person; and in his days as vicar of the university church of St Mary's, their devotion even went so far as imitation of his distinctive mannerisms of voice and gesture while conducting a service. Stereotypical portrayals of Keble as a saintly country parson, or of Pusey as the heroic leader of the post-1845 movement are widely found which similarly treat them as charismatic figures. In a later generation Edward King, bishop of Lincoln, was regarded as a saint during his own lifetime.

Leaders of religious communities such as Mother Lydia or Mother Kate were seen in terms of their distinctive attributes although these were not always appreciated, Mother Lydia in particular being regarded by some as a tyrant. A priest like Lowder of St Peter's, London Docks, gained a holy reputation for his care of the sick during a cholera outbreak, thus acquiring the title of 'The Father'. His successor Father Wainwright was considered 'an authentic saint of God'.[25] Victims of the ritualistic persecutions such as Father Tooth of St James', Hatcham, and Father Mackonochie of St Alban's, Holborn were both turned into martyrs with monuments: Mackonochie's in the 'Mackonochie chapel' at St Alban's and the memorial at the place where he died in the Mamore forest, Tooth in the 'Hatcham crucifix' (apparently of dubious provenance) and his vestments, both of which are now at Walsingham. Indeed the history of the Walsingham revival itself presents an excellent example of charismatic attribution, since it is often seen as Father Patten's achievement alone to have restored both Marian devotion and pilgrimage within the Church of England.

The presentation of particular priests in charismatic guise is common in the literature. Parish histories are often written largely in terms of the distinctive contributions made by a succession of priests to the growth of the Catholic faith.[26] This points to the strong association between the charismatic element in Catholicism and its tendency to clericalism. Although individual laymen such as Lord Halifax, Athelstan Riley, Sir Hubert Miller and more recently Uvedale Lambert and John Betjeman played a prominent part in the movement, the role of the clergy was always prime. This is not surprising once it is recognized that the movement was clerically pioneered and sustained. Parishes became Catholic because of the actions and policies of a particular vicar, and would remain so only if Catholic clergy continued to be appointed. Where there was a change of churchmanship with a new incumbent, parishes might experience sudden and violent shifts of orientation, with consequent changes in the congregation. Due to the oddities of the Anglican patronage system, there have been cases where a Protestant vicar taking over a Catholic parish has instantly destroyed vestments, crosses, statues and any other Catholic bric-a-brac he could lay his hands on, and opposite examples where a priest has gone from Matins to Solemn Mass virtually overnight, sometimes without protest, sometimes bringing about long-drawn-out struggles.

A second aspect of charisma to which attention should be drawn is the importance given by Catholic pioneers to what sociologists call 'charisma of office'. Personal charisma is ephemeral, since it attaches to a particular individual.[27] It has to become routinized in some way if the movement is to persist. A line of succession must be designated by heredity or some other means. In the case of the clergy, of course, the obvious criterion is the apostolic succession, the standard textbook example of routinized charisma and a central theme in Tractarian theology.

Thus within the Catholic movement, two types of charisma are to be found. Personal charisma was clearly important as a source of social influence during the early period of the movement, and has been evoked since on many occasions to explain, justify and elevate the nature and conduct of particular individuals. Dependence on personal charisma may have been greater then than at present, but remains latent and may appear from time to time. Office charisma was inherent in the movement because of the doctrine of the apostolic succession, and was particularly stressed by the Tractarians as a way of strengthing the Church against what were seen as secular, political and ideological attacks.[28] Against the threat to tradition presented by widespread scepticism, political instability and liberalism, the Tractarians asserted the existence of a spiritual authority underpinning leadership roles within the established Church, thus seeking to differentiate it from the institutions of the wider society, and especially from the state.

A final aspect of office charisma important to Catholics was the means it provided of drawing a distinction between the personal qualities of the individual and his organizational role. Such personal qualities may not always be attractive–sometimes just the opposite–but office charisma renders them irrelevant. The distinction can be employed to suggest that although a parishioner may not like Father so-and-so as a person, this does not affect his position as vicar, priest or father in God. A similar point is made in the Articles of Religion where it is stated that the 'unworthiness of the minister ... hinders not the effect of the sacrament'.[29] In this way an attempt can be made to retain loyalties which might otherwise be alienated by personal antipathy. Such a use of the charisma of office is a convenient (though not always effective) device for controlling potentially destructive interpersonal conflicts. It is sometimes linked to the concept of *alter Christus*, which states that, whatever the priest may be like as a person, when he is performing priestly functions he stands in the place of Christ. Again, this is a useful way of retaining loyalty to belief, practice and institution despite personal hostility, though the notion of *alter Christus* can sometimes have the not altogether unsurprising effect of increasing clerical self-esteem.

The Church within a Church

At the height of the movement Anglo-Catholicism became to a large extent a closed social world, whose members were able to live as if the Anglo-Catholic conception of religious belief and practice was all-sufficient and all-embracing. Of course they knew themselves to be members of the Church of England; and they were mostly aware that outside the Catholic world there existed, within the same Church, other worlds which sharply differed from their own (though not in all cases: I have spoken to some people brought up in a strong Catholic tradition who at least until their teens were unaware of any alternative in Anglican worship to High Mass on Sunday morning and Solemn Evensong and Benediction on Sunday evening).

When Anglo-Catholics prayed for 'the conversion of England', they sometimes meant the conversion not merely of the unbeliever, or even of the non-Anglican, but also of those Anglicans who did not share the Catholic viewpoint. This attitude still persists, drawing accusations of bigotry and extremism, though presumably it is quite valid (if not always tactful) for those who accept Catholic claims. At High Mass in a theological college ordinands were regularly heard to pray during the intercessions for the conversion of their diocesan bishop to the Catholic faith, illustrating the familiar point that the best way to heap coals of fire on an opponent's head is to pray for him.

Anglican Catholicism in its triumphalist phase has been described by one writer as follows. 'Guarded by the freehold and an antiquated machinery of clerical discipline, Anglo-Catholic vicars were virtually bishops in their own parishes.

The curates and nuns were their diocesan staff; the Parochial Church Council was regarded as an unnecessary evil ... The official diocese was viewed with indifference, suspicion, or even hostility ... the High Church layman could spend the whole of his worshipping existence in the parishes of his own tradition ... As for the Anglo-Catholic ordinand, he joined the Anglo-Catholic society at his university, went to an Anglo-Catholic theological college, prepared for his ordination examinations by reading Anglo-Catholic books, served his title under an Anglo-Catholic vicar, was appointed to Anglo-Catholic parishes, and, when he died, benefited from all the last rites that Anglo-Catholicism was able to offer him. Comprehensiveness was anathema. He was a party man through and through. Not even the Church of Rome in its most illiberal, ultramontane days shielded its children more efficiently from Evangelicalism, modernism, radicalism, or whatever other -ism was threatening the peace of the Christian fellowship.'[30]

Anglican Catholics might seek to create within the Church of England a religious community which was sociologically comparable, in terms of authority, cohesion and practice, to that of the Church of Rome, but the different history, structure and membership of the Church of England made this a virtual impossibility. However secure the 'Church within a Church' seemed, it remained part of a pluralist institution. An unquestioned legitimacy could not be attained since there were always challenges to it from other Anglicans, from Parliament and the episcopate, from Roman Catholicism and from militantly anti-catholic sources. Thus there has always been a series of dilemmas for some Anglo-Catholics, who have experienced constant mental and social pressures as a consequence of the tension between their strong commitment to the Catholic faith and the nature of the Church within which they attempted to express that faith. Such people seek the 'perfect society' which members of religious protest movements are always in search of, and cannot find it in the Church as it is. They therefore have to decide whether to stay or to go, to protest from within or from without.

The Anglican Catholic movement is an example of the sociological form which Joachim Wach called the *ecclesiola in ecclesia*[31], the group formed within a Church to protest against compromise and laxity. It therefore shares the problems of such groups. The term derives from the Pietist Spener, who himself attempted to bring about change *within* Lutheranism.

But his views offered the basis for a separatism founded on his criticism of the Church, and in Lutheranism secession did follow, partly based on Spener's ideas. Anglican Catholicism has from the outset displayed a tension between the aim of revival within the Church and secession, either individual or collective. Secession may be to the Roman Catholic Church, or to a new Church to be founded by the secessionists, and occasionally to Russian or Greek Orthodoxy. The latter has become more popular since the 1960s, when Rome itself became 'protestantized' to some extent following the second Vatican Council. In each case the attraction is to a Church embodying those beliefs and practices which are thought to be sadly lacking in the Church of England. The growing popularity of Orthodoxy is no doubt due in part to its refusal to bow to current fashion, and to its strikingly numinous liturgy.

3

The Meaning of 'Catholicism'

I believe with a conviction the intensity of which I can hardly express, that it is . . . the God-given vocation of the Church of England to realize and offer men a Catholicism which goes behind the Reformation in real and unimpaired connection with the Catholicism of the past . . . which is Scriptural and represents the whole of Scripture; which is rational and can court the light of all genuine enquiry; which is free to deal with the new problems and wants of a new time while it does the old work of conversion and sanctification; which acknowledges the authority of its ministry, but an authority constitutional, not absolute; scriptural, not arbitrary.

Charles Gore

The ideological diversity within Anglican Catholicism is one of the key factors in understanding its patterns of development and consequent influence. The Catholic party came to contain a broad range of attitudes, opinions, beliefs and practices which reduced its cohesion and solidarity, thus adding to the fragmenting effects of clericalism, congregationalism and individualism. Indeed the individualistic element was expressed in what came to be known pejoratively as 'private judgement'. This was of significance in itself as indicating a departure from norms of Catholic authority and church order, and the fundamental absence of a unifying source of authority which could promote greater cohesion. Some Anglican Catholics located authority in the traditions of the Church of the first five centuries, others in the 'Anglican tradition', others in the Roman Catholic Church. And the absence of a common view on the locus of authority was closely related to the lack of a consensus on the meaning of the term 'catholic', the foundational idea of the whole movement. Such a consensus was sought, indeed its recovery was a central aim of the Oxford Movement, but it was not achieved.

The Tractarians

The political concerns which gave rise to the movement of 1833 – the concern with the temporal state of the Church and the secular threats to its authority – were the trigger for a movement of religious reform which tried to set before the minds of men a vision of the true (i.e. supernatural) character of the Church and the authority which it embodied. The problem as seen by one of the participants in the Hadleigh house party of July 1833 was that there was 'no principle in the public mind to which we could appeal; an utter ignorance of all rational grounds of attachment to the Church; an oblivion of its spiritual character as an institution not of man but of God; the grossest Erastianism most widely prevalent especially among all classes of politicians'.[1] And it was this deficiency which the Tractarians sought to remedy. But they disagreed in some matters from the outset, and in the course of the next century and a half their successors were to take a variety of routes towards the public understanding of the nature of 'the Catholic Church'. In general there was a move, paralleled in other schools of thought, religious and secular, away from the proclamation of a dogmatic objectivism and towards a stress on the subjective which the Tractarians themselves had clearly rejected.

And yet there was a tension *within* Tractarianism: the romantic elements in its ideology pointed towards experience in a way which was formally rejected. For the authors of the Tracts, the immediate political problem was seen as arising from a more fundamental ignorance of the divine character of the institutional Church; solutions were to be found in setting out anew the rational grounds for recognition of this fact. But the Oxford Movement was also a movement of the heart, a mystical vision which transcended the mundane arena of politics, and the nature of its appeal was affective and poetical as well as rational. Vidler captures the vision in striking terms. 'It was as if the Tractarians were declaring that on the drab, dirty, and distempered walls within which English churchmen were wont to worship or to doze, there were wonderful pictures that, when uncovered, would transform the whole building into something mysterious and sublime. That such a transformation of the Church might take place was the possibility that began to haunt and charm the minds of many who read the Tracts for the Times. As the series advanced – ninety Tracts in all were published – one aspect after another of the Church's rites and institutions that had seemed dead or obsolete began to glow with new meaning.'[2]

The experience as Vidler describes it is one which has been shared by many subsequent converts to Anglican Catholicism: suddenly seeing the tired, shabby and familiar Church of England as guardian of a sacred tradition which they thought was no longer to be found. This tradition is given the title 'Catholic'.

Broadly speaking, 'catholic' has been used in two senses when applied to the Christian Church. Firstly the Church is thought of as *universal*: it includes (at least potentially) all the peoples of the world regardless of race, colour, creed or any other secular division. Secondly the Church possesses *doctrinal orthodoxy*: there is a consensus of belief. Both these elements come together in the frequently cited formulation of St Vincent of Lérins, 'what has been believed always, everywhere and by everybody' (*quod semper, quod ubique, quod ab omnibus*).

In this light the Church becomes a unique and extraordinary institution, which throughout the long centuries has held true to the faith delivered to it by its founder, embodying that faith in every conceivable way: teaching, worship, spirituality, architecture, the arts, law, philosophy, and all aspects of social life. Where other forms of Christianity are partial, narrow and limited, Catholicism offers a complete integration of the whole of human experience. This view may be contrasted with other conceptions of the Church which were current in the nineteenth century.

The Protestant conception was of a Church as essentially an assembly of like-minded people, a fellowship of the elect. There might be considerable variety and division within the Church, and the groups thus created might be linked in a loose 'federal' structure, but no special form of organic unity was considered obligatory. Alternatively there was the Erastian conception, deriving its name from the sixteenth century Swiss theologian, Thomas Erastus, who held that in a state with one religion, the civil authority has jurisdiction in all matters, whether civil or ecclesiastical. With regard to the Church of England, this approach was employed to argue that since the Church had been established by the law of the state, it must be subject to that law and could not be an autono-

mous body. Thirdly, there was the Catholic conception, but at
the time this was limited in two ways: it was applied largely to
the Roman Catholic Church, and, reflecting the religious
conflicts of the Reformation and after, it frequently carried a
pejorative sense: Catholics were thought of as corrupt, superstitious and worldly.

The Tractarians and their successors reasserted the Catholic
nature of the Church of England and gave this a very positive
meaning. Against the Erastians they argued that the Church is
not merely a branch of the state, but a divinely founded institution which is sacramental in nature. There was no break at
the time of the Reformation, but rather a continuity with the
Church founded by Christ; the Church of England is part of
'the historic Catholic Church of the ages'. Against the
Protestants they argued that there is only one Church, which
possesses organic unity, and the Church of England is part of
that Church; a 'branch' of the universal Catholic Church as
some Anglican Catholics were to put it later. Thus the
Protestant 'federal' conception must be rejected.

According to the Tractarians there should be 'reserve' in
communicating religious knowledge. The Church preserves
religion as a sacred mystery, the teaching of which is not to be
treated lightly or vulgarized. The truths of the faith are
embodied in scripture, the creeds, and the traditions of the
Church. They are transmitted through the three-fold order of
ministry – bishops, priests and deacons – which is grounded in
the apostolic succession, the direct and unbroken link with
Christ as founder of the Church. At the heart of the Church's
life are the sacraments, especially Baptism, by which new
members are incorporated into the Church, and the Eucharist,
where Christ is present in some sense in the bread and the
wine of the Holy Communion. Such a vision of Catholicism the
Tractarians and their successors attempted to set out and
defend.

The foundation of all Tractarian teaching is the notion of
authority. This authority comes specifically from the apostolic
succession, the direct and unbroken link between the apostles
of the first century and the bishops of today. More generally,
Catholic authority is grounded in tradition. The appeal to
tradition is often employed as a device for coping with the
insecurities generated by rapid social change; among the
Tractarians it was especially articulated by Keble. Tradition
must be preserved, and of all ancient institutions, the Church
is supreme. Moreover, it functions as a guide to the interpreta-

tion of revealed truth. That truth is contained in the Bible, and
the Church can neither add to nor contradict it; but it is a
profound truth which can only be fully understood by the
person who has experienced an increase of grace through
sharing in the life of the Christian community, learning from
its teachers and obtaining sanctifying grace through its
teachings and sacraments. This places the Church at the centre
of the Christian way of life.

As a model of what the Church should be, Keble looks back
to the patristic age – in other words he seeks out not merely to
preserve tradition, but to use it to bring about what Newman
called 'a second reformation', and what here we are calling a
'revolution by tradition'. In Keble's words, 'Is there not a hope
that by resolute self-denial and strict and calm fidelity to our
ordination vows, we may not only aid in preserving that which
remains but also may help to revive in some measure, in this
or some other portion of the Christian world, more of the
system and spirit of the apostolical age? New truths, in the
proper sense of the word, we neither can nor wish to arrive at.
But the monuments of antiquity may disclose to our devout
perusal much that will be to this age new, because it has been
mislaid or forgotten, and we may attain to a light and clear-
ness, which we now dream of, in our comprehension of the
faith and the discipline of Christ.'[3] From this conception of the
authority of tradition there followed an attempt to encourage
the wider reading of the Fathers, by publication of their
writings in English. Also, recognizing that tradition is not
merely static, a theory of development was discussed especially
by Newman.[4]

The second keystone of Tractarian thought is the doctrine of
faith. The note struck is anti-rationalist: faith is not, as Paley
and others had taught, an intellectual response to the rational
evaluation of evidence, but rather a gift of God, which comes
by hearing the teachings of God as presented by the Church,
and by accepting them on faith alone. This response is a
product of conscience: the individual is faced with the need to
live and to act, and must decide in which way he shall do so;
he has certain hopes and desires, and makes the leap of faith
in the direction which his conscience indicates. To say this is
not to reject evidence or reason utterly, but to assign them a
secondary place, a confirmatory role rather than one of initial
proof. What comes first is moral judgement and religious feeling, acted upon by the grace of God. The safeguard against
superstition or error in making the decision of faith is not

reason – to apply reason to such sacred matters is to profane them – but a right state of heart, a movement of love, perfected by obedience to divine commands.

The conceptions of the holy character of the Church, the divine nature of the priestly calling, the life founded in faith and strengthened through the sacraments and through sanctifying grace, all rest on the Tractarian version of authority. One final component needs to be noted in this summary of the thought of the Oxford Movement: the mystical stress. This is found in the Tractarian approach to the Eucharist, in the teaching of the doctrine of the real presence of Christ in the elements of the bread and wine. This doctrine was set out with some caution at first, though both Pusey and Keble were to become more definite in their later statements on the subject. It formed a focus of conflict throughout the nineteenth and early twentieth centuries.

The Eucharist, in Keble's words, calls for '. . . a special adoration and worship in the heart of everyone seriously believing a special, mysterious presence of Christ, God and man, expressed by the words, *This is My Body* . . . For the true oblation in the Eucharist is not the Bread and Wine – that is only as the vessel which contains or the garment which veils it; but that which our Lord by the hands of the priest offers to His Father in the Holy Eucharist, is his own Body and Blood, the very same which He offers and presents to Him – with which, as St Paul says, He appears before Him *now*, night and day continually – in heaven, in commemoration of His having offered it once for all in His Passion and Death on the Cross.'[5]

The mystical component is also present in Pusey's teaching that life must be a matter of daily obedience to the will of God, and in his idea of the Eucharist as the gate through which the divine presence enters the soul. Pusey was responsible for many of the translations of medieval mystical writings which began to appear about this time, and he gave practical expression to his spiritual concerns as an advocate of, and adviser to, the revived monastic life in the Church.

Taken together, these beliefs constitute what may be called 'Tractarian Catholicism'. In using such a term, I do not wish to suggest a level of systematization which did not exist in reality: elements were separable and would be given varying stress by different groups and individuals. Here again the potential for fragmentation is apparent. But with this qualification, such beliefs offer a powerful set of propositions by which the religiously-minded person may understand and live his life.

Sociologically their implications are profound: they specify a range of responses to nineteenth century British society which are in opposition to the established order at a number of levels. The potential for conflict is considerable. And it was to be realized in full measure by the Tractarians and their successors.

The effects of Tractarianism should not be thought of only in theological terms. Crafts, music and architecture were all stimulated by its ideas. The Catholic revival produced an extensive literature, including poetry and fiction as well as theology and philosophy, and the impact of Tractarian ideas is as apparent here as it is directly in the life of the Church. Writers influenced by Catholicism, Anglican or Roman, possessed certain distinctive features, as Raymond Chapman suggests. 'What is characteristic of the writers whose motivating force was a rediscovery of Catholicism? Their devotion was strong, directed towards a vision which had become clouded by concentration on immediate issues, formal worship and socially acceptable religion. There is distress and torment too. Patmore finds a unifying calm, but the happy confidence of Chesterton and the arrogantly hearty faith of Belloc were yet to be. To commit oneself, to venture on ecstasy, seemed to call for renunciation. The poets played their part towards a more sensuous apprehension of worship; yet the prevailing puritanism of the Evangelical spirit kept its hold even on those who had a different view of faith. The devotional manuals which appeared in large numbers towards the end of the century often combined ritualism with the stern perfectionism of Law and Wilberforce. Those who took religion really seriously did not know the meaning of compromise: that was their strength, sometimes their tragedy.'[6] Some critics might say that the modern successors of the Tractarians know only too well how to compromise both with institutional forces and with those of the wider world.

Liberal and radical Catholicism

There was no single version of Catholicism; its meaning was worked out in a different and more critical fashion in the liberal Catholicism which appeared in the work of Maurice, Gore, and other writers towards the end of the nineteenth century. The Tractarians had seen Catholic Christianity as founded on the great theological ideas developed during the early centuries, and on an unbroken tradition expressed through dogma and rite. Scripture, tradition and liturgy were joined by them in a unified and objective conception of faith. They might have taken a different route: Pusey had for a time wrestled with the emerging German biblical criticism which was willing to consider the place of myth in scripture, and the nature of the sacred texts as human products; but he was to disown this early phase in his career, to turn his back on such dangerous ideas and, as Cupitt sees it, to retreat into orthodoxy.[7] Later thinkers were less cautious.

F. D. Maurice rejected the rigidities of Tractarian orthodoxy; he was highly mistrustful of systematized theological schemes and systems and of the consequences of ecclesiastical parties. He preferred to concentrate on the gospel, which for him pointed centrally to Christ, through whom men are to discover God and their neighbour. This was the foundation of his 'Christian socialism'. Towards the end of his life, in 1860, there appeared a collection of essays by seven Oxford dons, *Essays and Reviews*, which attracted considerable attention. Though not especially radical by modern standards, they introduced a wider public to some of the ideas of the continental critics; for example, the problem of how to justify the use of scripture to prove a doctrine in the light of problems of interpretation. The work was highly controversial, and two of the authors were tried for heresy, though finally acquitted. The older Pusey saw the writers of *Essays and Reviews* as expressing a 'random dogmatic scepticism' and discarding many central doctrines 'in their ordinary if not plain, sense'. If the authority of scripture and the Church is doubted, he argued, the Catholic movement will face enormous problems of apologetics in the future.

Thirty years later another collection of essays, *Lux Mundi*, (1889) edited by Charles Gore, was published. All the contributors were Anglican Catholics who accepted the implications of biblical criticism and idealist philosophy. They sought to present the Catholic faith of Anglicanism in a manner appropriate for their time. Gore's essay on 'The Holy Spirit and inspiration' and Scott Holland's on 'Faith' attracted most attention, and again a furore arose. Gore in his essay took a line which to some such as Liddon seemed to be a capitulation to a highly individualistic form of criticism. The authority of the Church was discarded, Liddon argued, and replaced by the individual reason treated as 'an absolutely competent and final judge'. A kenotic Christology was offered, according to which, in becoming man Christ gave up divine attributes such as omnipotence and omniscience. It was suggested in the light of critical approaches that he was to be regarded as a real man during his time on earth, not the purely superhuman figure of some theological presentations and popular piety. Gore was in fact rather more conservative than some of the contributors to *Essays and Reviews*; although he was influenced by evolutionary ideas current at the time, he saw a continuity between the biblical writers and the ideas of the modern world. In contrast, contributors to the earlier collection has seen a clear disjunction between past and present; this offered the possibility of considerable innovation, and thus was more radical in its implications.

Gore was a leading figure in the development of a liberal Catholicism. He held many of the views which are taken to be typical of liberalism: an openness to critical thought, if with certain reservations; a concern with 'the truth' wherever it is to be found, even in other religions; and a stress on the ethical implications of Christianity which were closely linked to his own version of Christian socialism. According to Gore, the most useful contribution which the Church of England could make to the world was the development of a liberal Catholicism, which he took to be the essence of Anglican theology. He defined it as 'in real and unimpaired connection with the Catholicism of the past ...–it is Scriptural and represents the whole of Scripture ... rational and can court the light of all genuine enquiry'; it 'is free to deal with the new problems and wants of a new time while it does the old work of conversion and sanctification'; it 'acknowledges the authority of its ministry, but an authority constitutional, not absolute; scriptural, not arbitrary'.[8] Gore stated that 'I mean by Catholicism ... not merely or primarily a doctrine of salvation to be apprehended by individuals, but the establishment of a visible society as the one divinely constituted home of the great salvation, held together not only by the inward spirit, but also by certain manifest and external institutions'.[9] He also claimed that 'Catholicism is not primarily one particular set of doctrines or one particular kind of ceremonial, but a supernatural fellowship in Christ'.[10] The central elements of 'a Catholic society' according to Gore were 'the succession of bishops, who with their assistant officers were the ministers of the word and of the sacraments'; 'the faith of the Church expressed ... in the Creeds'; and 'the canon of Scripture ... formed in order that the Church might be kept constantly in touch with the original revelation, on the maintenance of which its healthy life depended'. The sacraments were thus subsumed under the ministry – in itself an interesting categorization – though occasionally Gore treated them as a separate element.[11]

Because of his acceptance of the principles of rational criticism, Gore was accused by Lord Halifax of basing faith on private judgement and of being 'a Protestant free-thinker'.[12] G. L. Harvey said that 'in Gore, as in the Liberal Catholicism which traces back to Gore, there was a strong, though unavowed element of Protestantism'.[13] Insofar as Gore undoubtedly saw private judgement as in his own words 'a duty' in relation to matters of critical enquiry, this is fair comment. Gore was also quite ready to argue that 'Catholic and Evangelical ideas are both necessary in the Scriptural idea of the Body of Christ'.[14] Thus the linkage of the two apparent opposed elements within Anglicanism is again asserted.

But Gore's critical approach had its limits: he was prepared to regard the Old Testament in such a light, but maintained that the New Testament was to be treated as a reliable historical record.[15] In this he was less radical than some of his contemporaries. Similarly, though, he thought of himself as a Christian socialist, his attitudes were far from revolutionary in a political sense – he rejected the ideas of Marxism and saw the extent of possible social change as limited by fundamental psychological and social constraints.

A further liberal publication was *Essays Catholic and Critical* published in 1926, thirty seven years after *Lux Mundi*. It was a collection by fourteen Anglican writers based on Cambridge rather than Oxford, influenced both by *Lux Mundi* and by Roman Catholic modernism. It sought to oppose the reductionism of some modernist and liberal Protestant theologians, and to present Catholicism as compatible with the methods of biblical and historical criticism. There was a greater stress on the place of experience in religious life than had been found either among the Tractarians or the *Lux Mundi* group, giving some weight to Liddon's fears, expressed forty-two years earlier, of growing subjectivism in the movement. Experience, it was argued, though it cannot be adequately dealt with by historical science, is nonetheless central to the religious life. Symbolism and ceremony are not merely means of presenting theological ideas, but are important in themselves as ways of expressing experience and thought more powerfully than words. Nor is experience to be thought of only as exotic; while mystical experience undoubtedly has a special place in the Christian life, religious experience *per se* is not for religious virtuosi alone, but for any person who is able to live up to the demands of Christian commitment. Much of this experience will inevitably be inarticulate, and will require expression through theology. According to Wilfred Knox experience provides a fundamental underpinning for belief: 'the Catholic faith is an organic whole, the truth of which is guaranteed more by its intrinsic value as proved by past experience than by the oracular infallibility of certain isolated definitions'.[16] And according to Milner-White, the Catholic Church is a powerful mediating agency for experience, which he sees as 'a Sacrament of Holy Spirit to the world'.[17] The quest for experience as a counter-secular device is now being openly stated as rationalist criticism bears harder upon a purely dogmatic stance; the way of re-enchantment (discussed in detail in the next chapter) here receives academic endorsement.

The liberal approach in Anglican Catholicism took diverse forms. There is a subterranean stream, beginning in the 1880s, which is more subversive than the liberalism of Maurice, *Lux Mundi* and *Essays Catholic and Critical*. Whether it remains Catholic is one of the intriguing questions about the ideological aspects of the movement. The Catholic socialist Stewart Headlam is the first representative of this approach. Headlam appears a liberal in his theology: he sat lightly to many favoured Tractarian themes, and advocated the cause of doubt in preference to blind obedience. He told his parishioners to question everything. Nothing should be taken for granted: this applied equally to the Old Testament, much of which he saw as mythological, and to the New Testament and the creeds.

Yet Headlam has been seen not as a liberal, but as a reformulator of the orthodox understanding of Catholicism, though he attempted this in ways which would have been totally unacceptable to the Tractarians. He certainly claimed to be a defender and exponent of the Catholic faith, but his account of this was quite unlike that of any of his contemporaries, and has contributed to his reputation as an eccentric individualist. Whereas other Catholics defined Catholicism in terms of the apostolic succession, the three-fold order of ministry, the authority of scripture and tradition, the sacraments, and reserve in the communication of religious knowledge, Headlam either said little about these components or interpreted them in a highly original fashion. The apostolic succession had been a key element in the call issued by the Tractarians and their attack on Erastianism, but Headlam said nothing about it. In all his attacks on Protestantism he did not defend the dignity of the episcopal office. While he despised the vulgarity of much popular Protestant religion, it was not because of any doctrine of reserve: the faith as he saw it was to be communicated to anyone. 'Newman wondered if it were wise for the masses to be taught the Nicene Creed; Headlam taught the Athanasian Creed to working-class atheists in Charles Bradlaugh's Hall of Science.'[18]

Headlam's position becomes clearly apparent in his opposition to Tractarian teaching on respect for authority. Athelstan Riley saw Catholicism as founded on this, and believed that without such a basis, Catholicism would degenerate into mere sacramentalism. According to Riley 'a Liberal-Catholic is simply a latitudinarian with certain sacramental opinions'. In arguing thus Riley stood in the main Tractarian stream; in arguing the opposite, Headlam showed himself to be a very unconventional Catholic indeed. According to him authority should be treated critically. People should 'question everything; take nothing for granted; prove, sift, test every opinion, however venerable, however cherished'.[19] Doubt was far better than blind obedience, whether to a pope or to a book. Much of the Old Testament he described as mythological, long before the contributors to *Lux Mundi* took a far more cautious line.

He rejected what he considered excessive supernaturalism, but believed that Christianity could be freed of such elements without abandoning orthodoxy. He was thus opposed to the efforts of liberals insofar as these led to the undermining and watering down of the Christian advocacy of social justice. He defended the creeds, not because they were philosophically valid propositions about God – he saw Christianity as a faith rather than a philosophy – but because they revealed God's character and taught his purposes for mankind. Thus he argued that the first phrase of the Apostles' Creed is intended not to assert the existence of God, but to teach that he is our Father. Similarly, the passages about Jesus are not be be seen as statements of historical fact but as descriptions of his character as lord, king, emancipator, saviour.

Headlam was a ritualist, but offered his own distinctive interpretations of the sacraments. Following in the footsteps of F. D. Maurice to some extent, he rejected both Tractarian and Evangelical teaching on Baptism, which depended on the view that because of the Fall human beings were no longer the children of God. Against the Evangelicals he argued that conversion was not necessary to re-establish the bond with

God, and against the Tractarians that this bond could not be broken by post-baptismal sin. Baptism does not effect a change in the recipient, but is a way of making plain what is already the case, that everyone is, and remains, a child of God. And in his teaching on the Eucharist, Headlam was even more radical, disagreeing with Maurice as well as the evangelicals and Tractarians. Certainly he was an ardent sacramentalist who insisted on the teaching of the 'real presence' of Christ in the Eucharist. But he did not take this to mean transubstantiation or a corporeal presence. The presence of which he spoke was spiritual. Thus he reversed the route followed by the Tractarians. And in general, whereas the Tractarians and their successors such as Liddon saw the sacraments as a super-natural interruption of the natural order, Headlam thought of that order itself as sacramental. The world is suffused with the sacred. God is present in it, not only in the Eucharist but in flowers, the dance, bread and wine. There are other sacraments than those of the Church.

We see in Headlam the development of a critical consciousness very advanced for his place and time. Is he correctly labelled a Catholic then? Was not his position rather one which combined high church liturgy and broad church theology? Was Riley right to describe the position he held as mere sacramentalism? The answer to these questions brings us to the heart of problems about the meaning of 'catholicism'. Orens argues that Headlam can be seen not as heterodox but as offering a new interpretation of orthodoxy itself. His claim seems to be that Headlam's theology was Catholic because it retained and drew strongly upon certain traditional doctrines while giving them a new meaning. If I follow Orens' argument, Headlam's 'catholicism' lies in his support for the tradition, even if that is reinterpreted. Critics might argue that the implication of this view is that the substantive meaning of 'catholicism' shifts according to context; like 'democracy' it becomes a term of approbation or condemnation with no fixed meaning.

A modern argument which is equally radical, and substantively similar in some respects, treating catholicism as a source of standards rather than a list of affirmations, has been developed in Rowan Williams' recent attempt to answer the question, 'What is catholic orthodoxy?'.[20] He proceeds from a discussion of the essential features of orthodoxy *per se* to a consideration of Christian orthodoxy and finally of the *differentia* of the catholic version.

Orthodoxy is the tradition of a community, its collective self-consciousness perhaps. It is composed of a distinctive vision deriving from the foundational events of the community, and the interpretations of this which are developed over time. Such a tradition is never unitary but inevitably involves debate and difference; attempts to reduce it to a single conformist ideology are distortive and result from attempts by interested groups to use it as a means of power over others. So orthodoxy possesses a critical potential; present belief and practice can always be related to the source of the tradition. 'Heresy' is seen as an unacceptable narrowing of the comprehensiveness of the original vision, rejected as a result of the critical processes built into the tradition.

Christian orthodoxy is to be assessed on the basis of its account of the ultimate nature of existence, particularly in the light of its central 'story'. This is concerned with the dynamic linkage of the negative and the positive, loss and gain, the rejection of Christ's message and the ascension of human life and death into a transhistorical reality. The significance of Christ's death and resurrection is to be realized anew in every generation. Every way of living is constantly under judgement from the foundational event, and so Christian orthodoxy continually subverts its own existence. And this is not just an intellectual matter: sacramental practice is central to Christian orthodoxy, and the Eucharist is an involvement: 'every Mass . . . is Holy Week'.[21] Belief provides appropriate ways of living (roles, statuses) which must be supported by 'a relatively stable background' of repetition, regularity of conduct, language and symbolic action. 'Any orthodoxy involves shared ritual enactments, crystallizations of the kind of life the ideology serves: the Christian sacraments, above all the Eucharist, show the believer engaged with and challenged by the source event of faith, engaging in "cross and resurrection", and so making the paradigm his or her own, making the life lived from the sacrament a reflection, a kind of translation of the paradigm. And so . . . every believing life becomes, in some measure, part of "orthodox tradition".'[22]

Catholic orthodoxy especially stresses the role of shared symbols, and of the living continuity in time and space demonstrated by the sacraments, the saints and the apostolic ministry. It involves an interplay between a constantly growing tradition of image and story, and the critical negation which prevents the tradition becoming a merely self-indulgent accumulation of detail. It offers a basis for the widening of horizons and the deepening of goals, and involves far-reaching contemplation of the gap between reality and our understanding, vision and fact, project and realization. Its formulations are acknowledged to be inadequate for the truths to which they refer. Inevitably, therefore, any formulation of orthodoxy must be provisional.

The difficulty in this approach is succinctly summed up by Michael H. Taylor.[23] Is it a redefinition of orthodoxy, to mean little more than paying attention to the tradition without necessarily agreeing with what it says? Or are the 'fundamental patterns' what used to be called 'essential doctrines'? And if so, what is the substance of Williams' argument? Is it a restatement of Catholic tradition in modern categories, or a reformulation which leads to a radical dilution of that tradition?[24]

Theory and practice

So far in this chapter I have outlined a number of versions of 'Catholic' or 'orthodox' belief. The aim of these accounts has been to indicate the diversity of content which the labels cover. I now turn to the question of practice. Any attempt to deal thoroughly with the social expressions of the Catholic ideology would be complex and highly detailed, so here I attempt only a general sketch of patterns. My assumption is that Catholicism provides a range of options which can be combined empirically in various permutations.

Clearly, despite the contrary opinion to be found in many theological dictionaries, 'Catholicism' has no agreed meaning, unless it is reduced to mere formulae such as adherence to scripture, creeds, historic ministry and sacraments. Also a formal discussion of this sort, while important in understanding the wider issues, gives no sense of the meaning to members–what they do with such labels, how they employ them to legitimate some actions and condemn others, how their lives are affected by their commitment to a Catholic identity. 'Catholicism' is first and foremost a set of attitudes and practices institutionally embodied in the Church of England. It is doubtful if many Catholics, asked to define what the term means or what they understand themselves to be, would go much beyond a few elementary generalizations such as are to be found in any high church leaflet. Many of the issues dealt with earlier in this chapter would be unknown to the majority (though quite often there are some members of a congregation who have a detailed historical and doctrinal knowledge). The meaning of being a Catholic is only the subject of extensive theorizing by a very small minority, especially these days; in the nineteenth century, since the basis of legitimacy for Anglican Catholicism had to be worked out and asserted, matters were rather different. But I want to suggest that in trying to understand Anglican Catholicism in any period, we should assume for most members of the movement 'the primacy of practice'. In Marett's aphorism, 'Religion is not so much thought out as danced out': it is the *activity* involved in Catholicism which is important to most Anglican Catholics rather than its theoretical rationale.

Firstly, Catholic practice is found in elaborate and colourful church services. Sometimes these are the traditional High or Solemn Mass, Solemn Evensong and Benediction. But the degree of elaboration and colour may vary, and the rise of the Parish Communion and Parish and People movements in the post-war period has widened the gulf between Catholic teaching and Catholic ceremonial, as noted elsewhere. Thus it is often possible to find vestments and lights associated with a liberal or modernist theology.

In some cases the Catholic becomes obsessively attuned to a subtle code of visual and verbal signs. He is sensitive to terminology: 'Mass', 'Eucharist' and 'Communion' indicate a descending order of churchmanship. Is the rite Prayer Book, Anglican Missal, Series One, Two or Three, Rite A or B, *missa normativa*? How many candlesticks on the high altar? The 'big six' which so many Catholic clergy fought to get into their churches is suffering slow erosion: two stubby candlesticks, a freestanding nave altar, and a hanging Christus Rex are signs of modernity in liturgical fashion. Is the Blessed Sacrament reserved, a small white light, (preferably an atmospherically flickering candle rather than the dull glare of electricity), burning in front of it, and if so, in a pyx, aumbry or tabernacle? Are there crucifixes? Are they traditional and representational or modern, stylized and abstract? Does the church have statues of the Blessed Virgin and other saints? Are they decently small and obscure, hidden away on window sills in remote parts of the church, or vulgarly obtrusive, bright in the colours popularized by Faithcraft and prominently situated so as to be seen by the whole congregation? Are there prickets for the burning of votive candles? Is there a holy water stoup at the door? Do the clergy wear the clerical hat called a biretta, which they remove at certain points in services? This is seldom found today, though once it was a trade mark, along with the thirty-nine button cassock. Is the liturgy 'Sarum', based on the forms allegedly used at Salisbury Cathedral in the Middle Ages, with loose flowing vestments, or 'Western', patterned on Roman use and featuring the narrow 'fiddleback' chasuble? The Catholic takes note of the employment and frequency of genuflexion and bow; the use of the sign of the cross; the number of servers and the complexity of their liturgical performance; the degree of unity or disunity between clergy, servers and congregation, since Catholic clergy may be burdened by the unconverted; the use of prayers such as the Hail Mary or the Angelus; additions to the verbal order such as the *Orate Fratres* – (anglicized in a form such as 'Pray, brethren, that this my sacrifice and yours may be acceptable to the Father'); the existence of local cells of devotional societies and pressure groups such as the Church Union, Confraternity of the Blessed Sacrament, Society of Mary, Society of Our Lady of Walsingham, Catholic League or Society of the Holy Cross (known in abbreviated form as CU, CBS, SOM, SOLW, CL and SSC); the contents of pamphlet racks; notices of forthcoming retreats or 'quiet afternoons'.

All of these are clues to Catholic rectitude. The range of indicators has become steadily more complicated with the spread of liturgical change in recent years. An interest in such matters is often condemned as trivial, yet it persists, especially, though not only, among the clergy. Social scientists would not be so quick to condemn, since evidence from many cultures suggests that apparently trivial practices and interests embody deeply-felt meanings for members. The crucial personal and social functions of what to outsiders may often appear 'nonsense' should not be underestimated, as it often is, for example, in criticism of attachment to church buildings or established ways. Churchpeople who do this merely demonstrate an insensitivity to basic aspects of human nature.

Alongside such preoccupations are a range of commitments which ostensibly run deeper, and which are expressed in recognizable role types: the churchwarden who noticeably does not engage in any of the practices just described, but who faithfully attends services, meetings and social occasions, contacts newcomers and ensures that things run smoothly; the energetic ladies who clean the Church and arrange the flowers, but who, to the annoyance of the clergy, are then too tired to attend Mass; the devout ladies, sometimes grand with mantilla and exquisite ivory rosary, genuflecting, crossing themselves and bowing on every possible occasion, faithful supporters of every cultic event; the devout young men, often servers, who are similarly correct, though sometimes rather less faithful. Some of them will eventually become priests.

Less obviously, there are those of both sexes and all ages who through Catholicism have gained a deep sacramental belief, whose life evolves around the Eucharist, prayer before the Blessed Sacrament, regular confession and retreat. They are not so obtrusive, and their numbers may be declining, but they sustain the movement, giving it stability and persistence. On occasions, if they can be persuaded to talk about their beliefs, they reveal something close to pantheism: a conception of a sacramental universe in which natural objects contain and reveal the sacred, similar to that proposed by Headlam and Noel. This links up with a cluster of attitudes and practices which have been summarized by David Martin. He suggests that the celebration of Harvest Festival, Christmas and Easter contains a form of folk poetry which for some people is synonymous with being English. '... Catholicism is plausibly linked to all the idealization of Merrie England, the nostalgia for community, the reverence for timbered houses, the extraordinary vitality of the Gothic, and so on through endless derivatives which include the Folk Dance and Song Society, the Youth Hostel Movement, even the Society for the Preservation of Rural England ... what began as a movement to bring God back into the Church and to restore the concept of universal Christendom could end by finding him in an English garden.'[25] I shall develop this notion later in relation to the shrine at Walsingham.

This brings us back to a source of Catholic attitudes, Romanticism, especially in its rural form. Opposition to industrial society and its effects is a central ideological theme, whether expressed in the idealization of rural community, the search for alternative ways of life influenced by monasticism, or the belief that the political embodiment of Catholicism must be some form of socialism. In the last case, very much a minority option, Catholicism today joins hands with contemporary causes such as Marxism, feminism and racial equality.

4

Ritualism and Re-enchantment

> The loss of sacramental religion means the loss of faith in the Incarnation and at last loss of faith in the Creation. If you cannot find God in the Host you can find Him nowhere else. But if you find Him in the Blessed Sacrament then you must find Him suffering in the slums, hungry in the streets, in prison, denied in factories and offices. The whole of life is sacramental.
>
> *Raymond Raynes*

Rationalization and re-enchantment

A major theme in the sociology of religion has been the concept of secularization, which Bryan Wilson defines as 'the process whereby religious thinking, practice and institutions lose social significance'.[1] But we have to go beyond this in order to understand the complexity of the process (or processes) which allegedly have transformed modern industrial societies.

A well-known article by Larry Shiner[2] distinguishes six types of secularization hypothesis. In summary these are: (i) the loss of prestige and influence by religious culture and institutions; (ii) growth of a pragmatic concern with 'this world' rather than the supernatural; (iii) loss of religious influence over society; (iv) the 'naturalization' of religious ideas and institutions, so that they are seen as human products; (v) the 'desacralization' of the world, so that man and nature become the objects of rational-causal explanation and manipulation; (vi) the movement from a 'sacred' to a 'secular' society.

It immediately becomes apparent from consideration of this typology that secularization is a complex and multi-faceted phenomenon, and that it is theoretically possible for different processes to be proceeding at different rates, or working in opposite directions. We cannot *assume* a linear shift towards total secularity in any dimension, nor does evidence concerning such a trend in one dimension necessarily imply that a similar movement is occurring in other dimensions. Finally, to the extent that different dimensions exhibit conflicting patterns, we cannot assume a master trend; the reality may be incoherent. And this is not new. As David Martin pointed out in an early essay, in the Roman Empire might be found simultaneously people who 'maintain the old beliefs, adopt a modern scepticism, elaborate a religious philosophy like stoicism, participate in mystery cults, display increasing concern about astrology, and are converted to Christianity'.[3] We may at least suppose the possibility of a similar mixture in modern societies.

But at present I wish to concentrate on Shiner's hypothesis (v) – the desacralization of the world. It derives from Weber, who in the words of Shiner made the 'classical statement' of this view. He argued that trends towards 'increasing rationalization and intellectualization' mean that while one may not actually know how the world, or phenomena within it work, one *could* know: if we wish we can learn it at any time. There are 'no mysterious incalculable forces'; in principle one can master all things by calculation. 'This means that the world is disenchanted. One need no longer have recourse to magical means in order to master or implore the spirits, as did the savage, for whom such mysterious powers existed.'[4] Eliade has discussed a similar theme in *The Sacred and the Profane* (1961), as Shiner notes.[5]

Weber's notion of disenchantment (*Die Entzauberung der Welt*), and Shiner's concept of desacralization may thus be defined as referring to the elimination of magic from the world, the loss (or suppression) of a sense of the sacred, brought about by a growing rationalization, embodied above all in science, but to be found even within religion itself. Peter Berger spells out the historical pattern in some detail.[6] Disenchantment has been a major motif in Hebraic religion from the time of the prophets, who began the rationalizing trend by their codification of ethical precepts and their rejection of animism and orgiastic rites. In Berger's well-known aphorism, Christianity has been its own grave-digger because it has continued the rationalizing process begun in Old Testament times, especially through the forces let loose by the Protestant Reformation, although this has led to its own steady decline. The rationalizing effects of Protestantism are ultimately self-destructive.

Is it possible that there could be eventually a totally disenchanted society? For Weber this might appear to be so.

Weber's extreme pessimism is well known, especially his appraisal of the modern world: peopled by 'specialists without spirit, sensualists without heart; this nulity imagines that it has attained a level of civilization never before achieved'.[7] But ultimately, as Hill remarks, Weber leaves his options open and draws no definite conclusions.[8] However, there is considerable data to suggest that Britain today, like other modern industrial nations, is far from a secular society by the criterion of dis-enchantment. Magical and superstitious beliefs abound, and are documented in most elementary discussions of the sociology of religion. At the same time, orthodox religion retains a limited hold on the mass of the population: the overwhelming majority are passive believers, and about half are still occasional attenders at church services.[9]

However, Berger gives an important example of an opposite movement. In the medieval period, the form of Christianity dominant in Europe – Catholicism – was directly opposed to such trends. It combined a strong assertion of the trans-cendence of God with a qualification of that theme, through the conception of the Incarnation, and even more through its theoretical development in trinitarian doctrine. Catholicism thus reintroduced the notion of mediation between God and man, which was expanded to encompass a whole host of other mediators, angels and saints, culminating in the glorification of Mary as mediator and co-redeemer. 'In the measure that the divine transcendence was modified, the world was re-enchanted.' A radical rationalization was made unnecessary because of the comprehensive nature of Catholic piety and morality. The one contrary element in medieval Catholicism was its theodicy: the view of history as the realm of redemp-tion which ran counter to the static image of the Catholic universe, and which at the height of the medieval period was expressed not through the Church but through a variety of chiliastic movements. Catholicism, then, 'contains' secularizing impulses, but it cannot prevent them from breaking out again. The Protestant Reformation is precisely their re-emergence into the world, and the renewal of the rationalizing trend, the end point of which is modern secularity.

Berger, following Weber, opens up an important theme for the sociology of religion: the re-enchantment of the world. In more detail the conception seems to be as follows, using Berger's own terms and phrases. Compared to the 'fullness' of the Catholic universe, Protestantism appears as a radical truncation, a reduction to 'essentials'. Catholicism vastly increases the range of religious contents, bringing about an 'enchanted' world. The components of enchantment are most fundamentally 'mystery, miracle and magic'. There is an immense expansion of the scope of the sacred in reality. The sacramental apparatus is extensive, and is imbued with numinous qualities. The miracle of the Mass is central; less routine miracles are widely found. There is an immense network of intercession which unites the Catholic in this world with the saints and indeed with all departed souls. The world is ongoingly penetrated by sacred beings and forces. The sacred is mediated through a variety of channels – the sacraments of the Church, the intercessions of the saints, the recurring, miraculous eruption of the supernatural into everyday life.

If Berger's argument concerning medieval Catholicism is correct, it is reasonable to ask if this has been the only historical example of a reversal of the rationalizing thrust in Christianity. And can one argue that both disenchantment and re-enchantment are to be found in the historical record, and at the present time? Or is disenchantment – Shiner's desacralization – dominant? The answers to such questions are to be found by applying Berger's account of Catholicism to other potential sources of enchantment.

Recently sociologists have had much to say about the significance of the 'new religions' for the secularization debate. As Wallis[10] and others have pointed out, there are fundamental differences between these movements, and they cannot be treated as all engaged in a search for the sacred. They are often seen to operate at the expense of the established religions, and to have only marginal and unstable support. But some of them appear to provide further evidence that the public appetite for the supernatural and magical is far from dead.

Movements *within* established religions have had less attention.[11] Yet here too there is evidence of a continuing quest for the recovery of the sense of the sacred, a dialectic of the sacred and the profane. The theoretical significance of Catholic Anglicanism is precisely as a movement with the goal of re-enchantment. Weberian secularization theory envisages a linear process by which the world is progressively rationalized and disenchanted; Berger's modification points to an interruption of the process in medieval times. Anglican Catholicism is treated in this book as another interruption, especially in its ritualist guise. Within Catholic ritual, Christ is present in 'the mystery of wheat and wine'. Mary is evoked as 'our Lady', and she and the other saints act in the world in response to the intercessions of human beings. Churches are not just assembly halls but define a sacred space within which the holy is made manifest through ceremonial, vesture, music, incense. All these things come to pass, and are sustained, within an allegedly disenchanted world.[12]

A case study: Benediction

The general development of Catholic ritualism was outlined earlier. This was, of course, mainly focused on the recovery of the Eucharist as the central service of Christian worship, and its performance with all due colour and solemnity. Aspects of the recovery are discussed throughout this book. But to pursue the 'enchantment' theme another service, in which the element of mystery is dominant, will be studied. This is the highly contentious rite of Benediction of the Blessed Sacrament. Benediction is sociologically interesting because it carries Anglican ritualism to its most 'advanced' point, reveals differences of opinion with deep theological roots within the movement, and exemplifies the concern with 'mystery' and 'magic' which have been so much part of the Catholic ethos. Its decline in recent years illustrates the new pattern of 'disenchantment' apparent in postwar Catholicism.

Benediction is a service in which the consecrated wafer in which, believers hold, Christ is in some way present, is exposed on the altar in a 'monstrance'–an elaborate metal and glass case–and censed. Hymns, prayers, intercessions and litanies lead to the climax in which the officiating priest makes the sign of the cross with the monstrance over the kneeling congregation. It is unmistakably an act of adoration which to those who do not hold Catholic beliefs constitutes a form of idolatry, and which causes unease to some Anglican Catholics. In the nineteenth and early twentieth centuries, there was opposition to any such services. This was connected with objections to the reservation of the consecrated sacrament in an aumbry or pyx, its presence marked by a candle burning in a clear glass.

Hostility to both Benediction and reservation was related to the controversy over the doctrine of the real presence of Christ in the consecrated bread and wine of the Eucharist. As we have already seen in our discussion of eucharistic theology, Tractarian understanding of the doctrine underwent a process of development, culminating in belief in an *objective* presence, not one which was merely *spiritual*. There was considerable opposition to the doctrine in either form by Evangelicals and broad churchmen, who regarded it as unfounded and superstitious, and themselves believed the Eucharist to be no more than a memorial of the Last Supper.

Though initially cautious, Tractarians were prepared to affirm the real presence publicly when it came under threat. Pusey was delated to the Vice-Chancellor of Oxford for asserting it in a sermon preached in the university church in 1843, and was prohibited from preaching as a consequence. In 1853, Archdeacon Denison of Taunton was condemned by the Archbishop of Canterbury's court for stating the doctrine in sermons preached at Wells Cathedral. One of the best-known Tractarian statements is by Keble in his *On Eucharistical Adoration* (1857), where he claims that there must be 'special adoration and worship in the heart of everyone seriously believing a special, mysterious presence of Christ, God and man, expressed by the words, "This is my body".' W. J. E. Bennett declared that (I) 'myself adore and teach the people to adore Christ present in the Sacrament under the form of bread and wine, believing that under their veil is the Sacred Body and Blood of my Lord and Saviour Jesus Christ'. A further source of legitimacy was provided when Bennett's teaching was held not to be contrary to the beliefs of the Church of England by the Court of Arches in 1869 and by the Judicial Committee of the Privy Council in 1872.[13] But this did not end critical objections, which were to reappear frequently in the course of the following century.

Clearly reservation of the sacrament and adoration of the consecrated elements were bound to be a focus of controversy, if attempts were made to introduce them into the Church of England, in which substantial groups rejected their implications with horror. Benediction was widely seen as a decadent product of Counter Reformation Roman theology, unknown in the Orthodox Church and only achieving its modern form in Roman Catholicism in the sixteenth and seventeenth centuries. Critics argued that it was not justified by any reference to the Prayer Book, which indeed appeared to condemn such services, but was an innovation within Anglicanism only legitimated by reference to 'Catholic practice' as found in the Roman Church. It therefore provided evidence to support the recurrent fear of the 'Romanizing' element expressed both by non-catholics and by moderate high churchmen. The Catholic response to this was firstly to refer to the tradition of eucharistic adoration going back to the early Church, from which the liturgy of the Church of England was derived according to Tractarian scholarship – St Augustine had said that, 'No one eats that flesh unless he has first adored' – and to be found more recently in the teaching of seventeenth century divines such as Lancelot Andrewes who wrote that, 'Christ himself the reality of the sacrament, in and with the sacrament, outside and without the sacrament, wherever he is, is to be adored'. Secondly Catholics sought to show by an account of Prayer Book revision in the sixteenth and seventeenth centuries that though there had been different formulations in successive versions of the Prayer Book, an acceptance of eucharistic adoration was finally retained. Arguably 'acceptance' was too strong a term but it could certainly be so interpreted in advocacy of the Catholic view.

The black rubric at the end of the Holy Communion in the 1662 rite explicitly stated that 'No adoration ... ought to be done ... unto the sacramental bread and wine there bodily received, or unto any Corporal Presence of Christ's natural flesh and blood'. But the 1662 rite was the outcome of a long process of development and negotiation between groups holding different views. The 1549 Prayer Book had been relatively Catholic in tone and was sometimes used as a referent by modern Anglican Catholics. They pointed out that the 1552 revision had, at the inspiration of John Knox, introduced a 'doctrine of real absence' designed to encourage the reception of the sacrament sitting rather than kneeling, which latter practice Knox regarded as a 'diabolical invention'. In response to Knox's objections a new declaration was formulated which stated that no one need object to the practice of kneeling for Communion since no sort of adoration was intended: the Body and Blood of Christ were not there. 'It is not meant ... that any adoration is done, or ought to be done, either unto the Sacramental bread and wine, there bodily received, or unto any real and essential presence there being of Christ's natural flesh and blood.' But on the accession of Queen Elizabeth the English Prayer Book of 1552 was authorized to replace the Latin Mass in use under Mary, with changes in a Catholic direction including the omission of the black rubric. It was restored in 1662 in response to Presbyterian agitation, but in a form which denied only a 'corporal presence' rather than the previous reference to a 'real and essential presence'. (Allegedly this was the work of Dr Peter Gunning, later Bishop of Ely, who was strongly Catholic in his sympathies, and who apparently sought to reject a crudely materialistic view of the sacrament while implicitly asserting a spiritual doctrine of the real presence. It has also been attributed to John Gauden, later Bishop of Worcester.) The black rubric was again to become an element in negotiation over eucharistic doctrine in 1928, following the rejection of the Deposited Prayer Book in 1927, when an unsuccessful attempt was made to persuade Parliament that the proposed book was not 'Romish' in intention by inserting the rubric again in the Prayer Book order.

Once the adoration of Christ in the Eucharist is accepted as permissible, Catholics argued, then he may also be adored in the reserved sacrament. Again the early Fathers could be brought into play. St Cyril of Alexandria could be quoted: 'I hear that they say that the mystic blessing is of no avail for consecration, if it be reserved to another day. In so saying they are senseless. For Christ undergoes no alteration, neither is his holy body changed; but the efficacy of the blessing and the life-giving grace abide in it.' Doubts might be felt about the singing of the antiphon 'Let us adore for ever the most holy sacrament', since this appeared to be a flat contradiction of the black rubric and the specific condemnation of adoration by the Privy Council in 1872. But it could be argued that such condemnations rested on the definition of 'sacrament' as 'an outward and visible sign of an inward and spiritual grace'. The adoration of the outward sign could be rejected as idolatry, but adoration of the inward part – i.e. the 'thing signified' – could be justified as adoration of Christ himself, 'signified' in his body and blood.

The first recorded instance of the disputed practices occurred twenty-five years after Tract One. J. M. Neale began reservation at East Grinstead in 1857-58 and introduced Benediction in 1858. It is also known that Father Ignatius held a procession of the Host followed by Benediction on the feast of Corpus Christi in 1864.[14] However, no cases were reported by the Royal Commission on Ecclesiastical Discipline in 1906; attempts had been made to introduce it in parishes some years earlier, but according to the Report of the Commission, action by the bishops had checked this. One case of a service similar to Benediction was recorded at St Columba's, Haggerston, but this had not involved the exposition of the sacrament in a monstrance. The Report recommended that practices such as Benediction should 'forthwith be made to cease ... by the authority belonging to the Bishops and, if necessary, by proceedings in the Ecclesiastical Courts'. On the whole this advice was disregarded by bishops, but in one case in 1909, the Revd O. P. Henly of Wolverton St Mary (now Stony Stratford) in Buckinghamshire, was convicted by the Court of Arches of reserving the sacrament and giving Benediction. On 13 August in that year, he was physically excluded from his church. Two clerical representatives of the bishop, an inspector and police constables, were sent from Oxford to change the locks and keys on the church doors.[15]

The attractions of sacramental devotion were felt widely, even by those who were later to assume high office in the Church. The Revd F. Underhill, best known as Vicar of St Alban's, Birmingham, and to become bishop of Bath and Wells in 1937, had published a book in which he actually recommended not only the use of the Rosary but also Devotions to the Blessed Sacrament and Benediction.[16] His position moderated over time, and no longer represented trends in the movement, but this was not recognized by those in the episcopate who took him as a sounding board for Catholic opinion, and on this basis in 1928 sought to prune the proposed Prayer Book of some of its Catholic features.

By the late 1920s, Benediction was to be found in some form, solemn or simple, using monstrance or pyx, in a small number of churches. It was still highly controversial. For example, the Revd Sandys Wason of Cury in Cornwall was physically expelled from his parish by a group of angry farmers because of this and other such practices in 1918. In 1928, the House of Commons was debating the proposed new Prayer Book, a revision of that set out in 1927 to meet the feeling that existing practices were 'insufficient for the religious life of the nation'.[17] This had been modified in part to control the growth of Catholic sacramentalism. The proposed rubrics governing the reservation of the Blessed Sacrament were intended to be, in the words of one involved, 'watertight' against any extra-liturgical devotion, and considerable efforts were expended to make them so.[18] But Parliament rejected their proposals and chaos followed.

In October 1928 a Synod of the diocese of London, voted to reject the Bishop of London's proposal to follow the rules with regard to reservation. He then published a letter, dated 7 November 1928, which spelt out his rules regarding reservation and explicitly forbade Benediction and similar practices.[19] But his views were unacceptable to many London incumbents. Under Winnington-Ingram, London had become a stronghold of Catholicism, so he was partly responsible for the difficulties thus created.

At that time 149 London churches reserved the sacrament; 21 of these were prepared to reject their bishop's proposals in writing. In April 1929 they published an open letter in which they argued that since the Church of England is part of the universal Catholic Church, its members are entitled to avail themselves of practices which are part of the 'minimum of essential, fundamental belief common to them all. The Catholic doctrine of the Blessed Sacrament undoubtedly comes within the scope of this community of belief. On this hypothesis, therefore, we claim that our teaching and practice in no way go beyond that which has authority in the Church in the East and in the West.'

'There are wider aspects of the situation, and the controversy over the sacrament of the Eucharist is only the outcome of a much larger issue which lies behind it, namely whether or not the claim of the Church of England to be a part of the one true Church founded by Christ demands any practical recognition of our membership with the other parts of Catholic Christendom from which unhappily we are outwardly separated. For ourselves we cannot admit that the Church of England is an autonomous body nor forget that our position is abnormal.' The abnormality was seen as lying in two areas: firstly the lack of communion with every apostolic see – a reference to the Roman Catholic and Orthodox Churches; secondly the unreliable guidance offered by authority within the Church of England, due to the involvement of the state in making appointments to the episcopate.[20]

The Bishop responded in a letter dated 14 May 1929 that he was only prohibiting 'Devotions directly connected with the Reserved Sacrament. All I have forbidden you to do is to move the Reserved Sacrament from its appointed place, to open the aumbry or tabernacle, to cense it, or to allude to the Presence of the Reserved Sacrament in your prayers.' A correspondence in *The Times* followed, in which eminent figures in the Catholic movement such as Lord Halifax and Darwell Stone took the side of the twenty-one, while moderates such as Charles Gore and Francis Underhill criticized them for disobedience to lawful authority. The twenty-one responded to the Bishop with a detailed and scholarly letter justifying the position which they had taken, which the Bishop acknowledged while being unwilling to take the public correspondence any further.

In addition to disputes over eucharistic doctrine, what was at issue in the controversy over Benediction was partly the locus of Catholic authority, and partly the evangelical and teaching aspects of the service. With regard to the first, the Benediction disputes merely recapitulated earlier divisions within the movement; an enthusiastic minority took a papalist position, treating the Pope as head of the Catholic Church, of which the Church of England was a part though separated by historical accident. The majority of Catholics, however, for whatever reasons, were ready to defer to episcopal authority as then constituted in the Church of England, though the point at which they would do so exhibited some variation. Claims on the evangelical aspect can be illustrated from a sixty-page pamphlet on the subject published in the nineteen-thirties: 'once you show the Body of Christ to the people there comes a power of devotion which acts as an appetite and calls for more and more of what it craves. . . . Benediction is to satisfy the craving of the popular heart of Our Lord's own Blessing.'[21]

A far more subversive view of the significance of Benediction was taken by the Revd Conrad Noel, Vicar of Thaxted, Essex, and one of the leaders of Catholic socialism, discussed elsewhere in this book. As early as 1918, the Bishop of Chelmsford had objected to some of Noel's practices, including Benediction and the carrying, displaying and elevating of the consecrated Host.[22] But on the feast of Corpus Christi 1919, the Host was carried in procession in a monstrance from the church to the vicarage garden, and Noel announced that it would again be processed, and worshipped at Benediction for the midsummer festival on 28 June. He argued that he was merely reviving a ceremony traditionally approved and practised by the English Church. According to Noel, the 'Catholic rebels of the middle ages' carried 'Him' (the consecrated Host) in their midst, and 'celebrated their Red Mass on the field of battle'.[23] Noel did, however, admit under pressure the dubious legality of Benediction, and in Groves' words 'evaded' the question of episcopal authority by saying that obedience was impossible if the bishop held heretical views on the doctrine of the real presence. Watts Ditchfield, Bishop of Chelmsford at the time, denied the doctrine, holding that when Jesus said, 'This is my body', he was speaking figuratively. Noel's response was that, 'he who denies the doctrine forfeits the right to regulate the worship arising from it'.

The midsummer festival was advertised both in the *Church Socialist* and in the *Church Times* as follows: 'The Catholic Crusade welcomes all who wish to join in the Procession of the Divine Outlaw and to receive His blessing to encourage them in battle. Mere onlookers are not welcomed.' Not surprisingly, an invitation in such terms provoked a near riot. The procession took place amid scenes of pandemonium: the procession of the Host was guarded on either side by army officers against repeated attacks from protesters, and when, in Groves' words, 'for the first time in nearly four hundred years the Host was exposed and elevated to the people in Thaxted's main street', it was necessary to form a defensive ring to protect the ceremony against 'fresh and furious onslaughts'.

Benediction was advocated at a later stage in less dramatic terms, by Fr Martin Jarrett-Kerr CR. He reports the account of the Swedish Lutheran Professor Bengt Sundkler that, on a visit to Tanganyika in 1959, he had seen a congregation of a thousand Africans bowing before the monstrance at an Anglican church near Tanga, and had concluded that this was the practical Christian answer to the growth of Islam. Fr Jarrett-Kerr himself comments that, 'we cannot afford to forget the late Professor R. G. Collingwood's remark that in a world that has been atrophied by "amusement art", "the more magic the better" '.[24] One could hardly wish for a better statement of the re-enchantment theme in Anglican Catholicism.

Finally, so eminent a contemporary figure as John Macquarrie, Lady Margaret Professor of Theology at Oxford and an Anglican priest, has spoken of the emotional impact of the service on him personally, and its significance in transmitting an awareness of 'the sacramental nature of all creation' and its 'depths of meaning. . . . This act of devotion offers an important opportunity to renew our strength, and one wishes that its value were more widely appreciated in the Church . . . it is an enrichment of Christian worship and makes a valuable contribution toward building up the disciple in the Christian faith and life.'[25]

It is a profound irony that this service, the focus of so much past controversy, has been widely abandoned in recent years. Many Catholic Anglicans have either never heard of the service, or never encountered it, or regard it as merely a relic of the past. The political connotations seen by Conrad Noel have passed most people by. What was fought for, often at considerable personal cost, fifty years ago is now widely ignored. A different ethos, in which mystery is subordinated to a largely de-politicized understanding of community, prevails.

The history of Benediction illustrates the cross-pressures of feeling and doctrine within the Catholic movement. For an instructed congregation, Benediction is a powerful liturgical and doctrinal instrument. Yet it has been pushed to the sidelines by recent trends; ideology blunts psychological and social sensitivity, and clergy insecure in an age of decline are vulnerable to the pressures of fashion (as apparent also in the effects of the ideologies of ecumenism). Raymond Raynes once remarked that a first step to the conversion of England would be Exposition of the Sacrament on the altars of all its churches. Sociologically this view has force, but it has been given little attention in recent times. Instead, many clergy have followed secular fashion, looking to the east or to contemporary psychology and ignoring the sources already available within the Christian tradition.

Explaining ritualism

Ritual is a universal feature of social life. According to Robert Bocock,[26] ritual is 'the symbolic use of bodily movement and gesture in a social situation to express and articulate meaning'. He distinguishes four types: religious, civic-national, life-cycle and aesthetic. Ritual action is action oriented to objects set apart from the profane world. Bocock[27] particularly contrasts 'civic' and 'religious' ritual: the 'civic' form is to be found in groups of all kinds – national, local, educational, legal, political, even industrial.[28] All have ceremonies to mark special events, from a state visit to a retirement. What civic events in general do not have is a concern with the sacred or holy, and this is the distinguishing feature of the religious form of ritual.

The French sociologist Emile Durkheim has analysed its nature, social functions and psychological consequences. According to him, religious ceremonies are 'dramatic representations' comparable to 'games and the principal forms of art'. They involve the interpretation, elaboration and transformation of the real world; '. . . the world of religious things is a partially imaginary world, though only in its outward form'. This could be read as psychological reductionism, but Durkheim is clear that there is a distinction between the expressive and cognitive aspects of religion. Ritual may include actions which have no purpose and are purely expressive, but rites are not *merely* games or works of art: 'a rite . . . is part of the serious life'.

Rites arouse emotions which are perpetuated through the symbols of belief, and they generate communion by arousing individual sentiments which are fused into common sentiment. The religious cult is both 'a system of signs by which the faith is outwardly translated', and 'a collection of the means by which this is created and recreated periodically'.

Durkheim graphically locates the emotional power of religion. At the individual level, participation in ritual causes men to 'believe themselves transported into an entirely different world from the one they have before their eyes'. It is out of such experiences that 'the religious idea seems to be born', and through participation the 'conditions of psychic activity' are stimulated and advanced. The believer who has communicated with his god through ritual is a stronger man, who can better endure the trials of existence 'because he is raised above his condition as a mere man'.[29] It is precisely such consequences which gave strength to Anglican Catholicism.

Some religious ceremonies deal only with the symbolic representation of religious ideas; Catholic ritual, however, does not seek only to *symbolize* truth *but to give a living experience of it.* It is a drama, but, Catholics would claim, not merely a drama. The living God comes to the altar of every church in which Mass is celebrated, under the signs of bread and wine. It is this power which was let loose within the sober world of nineteenth century Anglicanism.

Sometimes the emotional effects could be overwhelming, especially on the young, as the following recollections by Norman Nicholson of an Anglo-Catholic childhood illustrate: 'Very soon I was passing through a phase of passionate, adolescent piety. I learned my catechism, renewed the pledges of my godparents and was confirmed. I knelt for long periods in my bedroom, praying and "preparing" myself for the next Sunday's communion. The thought of the moment of consecration could make me shake like a fever'.[30]

Anglo-Catholicism was undoubtedly of considerable importance in enabling a considerable number of people to deal with the variety of changes occurring in British society from the early nineteenth century onwards. A commitment to sacramental ritual was an effective defence for many against the insecurities thus produced. There is a sociological truth in the saying that, 'The sacrament does not only signify grace but also conveys it', as Durkheim observed.[31] Involvement in ritual became for participants a self-authenticating activity through which religion was living and change was manageable. The emotional power of ritual ensured that mere rationalism could safely be discounted.

Owen Chadwick gives four causes for the growth of ritualism in nineteenth century Anglicanism: taste, evangelism, congregationalism and obedience to authority.[32] There was an aesthetic motive. This was in part the outcome of the Romantic movement and its expression in the arts and architecture, and of the scholarship which was thus inspired. A need to put the newly discovered ideas into practice emerged and grew.

A common suggestion is that ritualism was, in Reynolds' words, a 'visual aid' employed by mission priests in slum parishes to teach Catholic doctrine to illiterate congregations. 'Finding, like Liddon, that the only way to get at the hearts of the poor was through their senses, they sought to set forth the glory of God and the beauty of holiness by means of ceremonial'.[33]

Ellis claims it was not until the ordinary man grasped the significance of the truths of the Catholic faith through the use of ceremonial that it aroused his loyal support, but he adds 'or, as was more usually the case, his undying hostility'.[34] And writing of a later period, Colin Stephenson observes that he thought initially that ceremony would attract people, but found by experience that it was more likely to drive them away![35] Ritual may have conveyed ideas; it did not always inculcate them.

The evidence on the effectiveness of ritualism in drawing people in is mixed. It was claimed to make a particular appeal to the working classes bringing colour into their otherwise drab lives. But Anglo-Catholics were handicapped in their evangelistic endeavours. As Hugh McLeod notes, the Anglo-Catholic priest sought to have the kind of relationship with his people which the Roman priest had automatically. He also wanted to recreate the kind of community which no longer existed in either town or country. Both these factors meant that the ritualists had an uphill task.[36]

We have some evidence from the eighteen-sixties. An agent of the Church Association reported only eight working class people in a full church (St Alban's, Holborn) on a Sunday morning, ten such people on Sunday evening, and on Wednesday evening eight poor men in a congregation of eighty odd.[37] But St Barnabas', Pimlico was said to draw congregations 'including many poor worshippers' to its services – up to 150 on weekday evenings.

By the early 1900s, social surveys[38] suggested that only a few Anglo-Catholic churches held the poor, though they did better than churches of other styles. Where this happened it could be numerically impressive – St Peter's, London Docks in 1902 had 884 attenders at morning service (but 584 were children under 15). Both Mudie-Smith and Booth thought that success with working men was due more to the enthusiasm and evident self-sacrifice of the priests than to their ritual. Masterman believed that the working man accepted elaborate ceremonial with resignation while finding it inexplicable, and defended it against Protestant attack through loyalty to the vicar more than because he cared about it.

In view of the claims made for ritual's attractiveness to the working class, it is ironic that by the end of the century, many ritualistic churches (though certainly not all) were clearly different in composition. There was a belt of well-attended middle class churches across south London – for example, St Stephen's Lewisham had 1,443 attenders, St Peter's West Norwood had 1,429. As Chadwick says, the movement's appeal seems to have been more to the devotional and aesthetic instinct of the educated than to the interest of the uneducated.[39]

A frequent observation is that Catholic congregations were (and are) eclectic: they constitute a community of interest. People belong to them because they like that kind of service. This pattern has been apparent from the 1860s onwards, with people travelling from all over London, and even in some cases from the suburbs, to attend churches such as All Saints', Margaret Street, or St Alban's, Holborn.

Eclecticism was encouraged negatively by the failure of some new urban churches to reach people in the locality, who often felt no sense of identification, and in some cases did not even know that they belonged to a given parish. The long-established parish churches still had their traditional congregations and experienced little or no conflict (St George's-in-the-East being an exception here). But most of the ritual churches where conflict occurred were new district churches composed of like-minded clergy and laity, and drawing on a constituency which did not coincide with parish boundaries. Such patterns were also apparent in some provincial towns, where full churches were to be found – for example, at St. Oswald's, Durham, or at Frome. Urban congregationalism has been both a strength and a weakness. It has encouraged internal solidarity and cohesion, but has also cut some parishes off from the wider life of the Church.

The importance of authority was highlighted by many aspects of Anglican Catholicism, in particular by clashes between clergy and bishops, and by the employment of the ecclesiastical courts to adjudicate in such matters. Catholic innovation was legitimated by reference to traditional practice, particularly the ceremonies and decorations ordered by the Prayer Book rubrics; and ritualism grew in part because the English respect for lawful authority strengthened the movement when it came to be believed that such authority, as represented by the Prayer Book, required such practices: the ceremonial laid down in Edward VI's first Prayer Book of 1549.

The resort to law by anti-ritualists did not always work as they hoped. When ritualistic conflict was at its height from the mid-1860s onwards, the Protestant Church Association pursued two goals: firstly, the employment of legal sanctions against ritualistic clergy, and secondly, a clear and unambiguous definition of church norms regarding the conduct of public worship. With regard to the first aim, the high points were the passing of the Public Worship Regulation Act of 1874, the long-drawn-out prosecution of Father Mackonochie from 1868-83, and the imprisonment for varying periods of five priests in the years 1877-87. The second aim found expression in the Ritual Commission of 1867, the Royal Commission on Ecclesiastical Discipline of 1904, and the Prayer Book controversies of the 1920s. These measures were of course not solely Protestant in inspiration; they also reflected the alarm felt by moderate sections of laity, clergy and episcopate at the threat to church order, as they understood it, which ritualism presented. But the outcome of all this activity was ultimately the opposite of what had been intended. Legal decisions legitimated much ritual innovation. Legal sanctions were disregarded by many clergy, and made martyrs of those who were imprisoned, thus assisting the Catholic cause. 'The blood of the martyrs is the seed of the Church', however small the sphere in which the martyrdom takes place. A similar effect was produced by mob violence and interruption of church services, though such conduct continued well into the twentieth century.

Thus, as the Report of the 1904 Commission made clear, ritualism in various degrees of extremity was to be found throughout the country. And it was to grow, in a climate of occasional furore (e.g. the 'battle against Benediction' after World War I), but also of advance and retreat in particular parishes, according to the inclinations of incumbent and parishioners. The high point was 1933, the centenary year; after that, a slow process of erosion set in, due to secular advance and ideological dilution.

Comments on Anglican ritualism by sociologists are very

sparse. Bocock discusses the liturgical reforms of the nineteen-sixties as a shift from 'mystery cult' to 'sacred community', and analyses the symbolism by which this is expressed. He gives an account of the forms of contemporary Catholic ritual and suggests that the Church of England has moved towards the 'Catholic' end of the spectrum since the end of the nineteenth century because Catholicism possesses a coherence previously lacking in Anglican thought, and appeals to 'intelligent and creative clergy and laity'.[40]

Bryan Wilson's view is different. According to him the nineteenth and early twentieth century ritualistic and liturgical revivals in both Catholicism and Anglicanism were no more than transient and unsuccessful attempts to oppose the dominant long term trends in western religion.[41] This view is perhaps rather one-sided. The Catholic revival has had far-reaching effects which are still with us today, bringing about extensive changes in both teaching and worship. It may be suggested as an alternative interpretation that Anglo-Catholic ritualism is in fact another example of 're-enchantment', to be placed alongside others which have occurred before and since. It brought back into the spiritually dry world of the Church of England at the beginning of the nineteenth century all the features of the Catholic form of Christianity which in Berger's analysis connote 'enchantment'. Rather than the linear decline which Wilson implies, there is peak and trough, and it is not clear that either will be ultimately dominant. However, a new trough has emerged as an unintended consequence of recent liturgical changes.

The new disenchantment

Anglo-Catholicism was counter-secular in a major sense. Particularly in its 'ritualistic' phase from the 1840s onwards, it tried to restore through its practice a sense of the Church of England as a spiritual institution rather than a department of state. As a novelist of the movement put it, 'The English Church, as established by the law of England, offers the supernatural to all who choose to come. It is like the Divine Being Himself, whose sun shines alike on the evil and on the good. Upon the altars of the Church the divine presence hovers as surely, to those who believe it, as it did upon the splendid altars of Rome'.[42]

Anglican Catholicism sought to achieve what in Weberian terms we may call a 're-enchantment of the world', a reversal of the secularizing process at the levels of both theory and practice. It was a major attempt to re-sacralize both a Church and a society which had already experienced extensive rationalizing forces. The aim was to create within Anglicanism an ethos which treated the world primarily as a battleground of spiritual warfare, constantly interpenetrated by the supernatural. Ritual was a vital form of praxis. This was because, as Mol has suggested, it has complex effects at a number of levels: expressing and supporting sacred meanings, creating and reinforcing group unity and integration, strengthening both individual identity and social bonds.[43] Anglo-Catholics might not speak in such terms but they had a clear sense of the social functions of ritual which Mol describes.

Anglo-Catholicism's appeal has been as much affectual as cognitive. On the doctrinal level it provided solutions to the problem of meaning by relating contemporary Anglicanism to its Catholic heritage and spelling out the implications for praxis in the contemporary Church. But the intellectual component would appeal only to a minority, other than in formulaic terms; the broad basis of Catholicism's support was quite different.

It is impossible to understand Anglo-Catholicism solely or even primarily as an intellectual movement. It was also the attempt to create a social world within which desired forms of religious experience would again be possible – a reaction not only to the pressures of social change but also to the inadequacies of the arid establishment Anglicanism of the early nineteenth century. The doctrinal issues over which battles were fought carry a heavy emotional charge which can only be understood in terms of a 'hidden agenda'. Catholics were engaged in a passionate quest for reality in religion – for authentic religious experience within the structures of a recovered Catholicism. But the attempt at recovery co-existed uneasily with a 'modernizing' and 'rationalizing' orientation present within British intellectual life in the nineteenth century and after. The tension between these two sets of factors could be controlled while external enemies were available in the shape of various militantly anti-catholic forces, but when these began to decline in virulence, the way was open for the co-option of moderate Catholics into the Anglican establishment, for internal dissension to weaken the anti-secular thrust, and for Anglo-Catholic solidarity, already limited, to be further undermined from within.

Both in their liturgical innovations and in their attempts to build up community within parishes, Catholics paved the way for the liturgical changes which have taken place in the Church of England since the 1930s. These embody ideals of both renewal and communitarianism, but also an often un-recognized ideological dilution. Clearly this was not the inten-tion when Fr A. G. Herbert published *Liturgy and Society* in 1935. Rather it seemed that the revaluation of the Eucharist, the greater solemnity and dignity of its presentation, and the increase in its frequency, all of which were attributable to the Catholic movement, were now to be made more widely avail-able. A slogan of the movement for liturgical renewal was, 'The Lord's own service on the Lord's day for all the Lord's people'. The members of a congregation were seen as the family of God in a particular place, meeting together on a Sunday morning to obey their founder's command, 'Do this in remembrance of me'. 'It is a joining of whole human families to offer the Great Sacrifice in order that they may be made into one supernatural family in the Church.'[44]

Hebert's writings, joined to those of Evelyn Underhill on *Worship* (1936), and especially to Dom Gregory Dix's *The Shape of the Liturgy* (1945), an enormously influential work of liturgical scholarship, were put into practice in the Parish Communion movement, which brought about a transformation of the pattern existing in the nineteen-thirties. The main Sunday service was no longer Matins or a Sung Eucharist (often non-communicating) at 11 a.m., but a Eucharist at 9 or 9.30 with general communion and congregational involve-ment. In a sense this was a further triumph for Tractarian ideas, but the stress on 'the family' was two-edged, offering a potential for 'secularization from within' as the Eucharist became a celebration of the human family, of which the Holy Family seemed often to be a pale reflection. In many churches the awe and solemnity on which the Tractarians had set such store was progressively lost amid a babble of voices, both from children compelled to endure an hour's 'participation' with their parents, and from adults using the occasion as a meeting with their friends rather than with God. The ultimate un-intended consequence of this has been the popular elevation of Christmas, as a folk festival of the family, to greater importance than Easter, a reversal of orthodox priorities which is clearly visible in Communion statistics over the last twenty years.

Further unintended change has been brought about by Prayer Book revision, which began with the establishment of the Liturgical Commission of 1955. This started a process of change culminating in the publication of The Alternative Service Book in 1980. The first eucharistic revisions were the two 'Series', 1 and 2, presented to the Church Assembly in February 1966, and increasingly used by churches throughout the late 1960s alongside the 1662 Prayer Book rite and various 'illegalities' ranging from the form rejected in the Prayer Book controversies of the late 1920s to the Roman Missal (itself also undergoing drastic change). The new services aroused familiar party antipathies. The Series 2 Burial Service foundered over Catholic advocacy of prayer for the departed and Evangelical objections to this. The draft Canon of the Eucharist–'we offer unto thee this bread and this cup'–appeared to imply a doctrine of eucharistic sacrifice which was unacceptable to Evangelicals, and was modified accordingly. And while some critics objected to the lack of contemporary English in Series 2, others regarded its language as greatly inferior to the sonorities of 1662.

A third series of alternative services came into use in the early 1970s. Series 3 employed modern language, most notably in addressing God as 'you', and was criticized for its linguistic poverty and absence of mystery. Defenders of the innovations argued that such comments were unjust, that familiarity would be necessary before they could be accurately judged, and that 'if worship was to be living and relevant, language had to make it so and must therefore not be archaic or remote from that with which people are familiar in their daily lives'.[45] Such comments are widely found, and contain a series of assumptions which are worth noting. The terms used – 'living', 'relevant', 'archaic', 'remote' – are emotive labels. Questions about the extent to which they may be fairly applied to either old or new services, and the actual consequences of those services in achieving what is claimed, are often unexamined.

In commenting on the petitions and other activities in defence of the Prayer Book which began in the seventies, Welsby suggests that, 'The signatories had little or no conception of the need for change which lay deep in the hearts of many churchmen, of the synodical processes whereby ordinary worshippers had been able to make their voices heard, or of the tradition of liturgical scholarship which had contributed to the revision of the services'.[46] Much of his claim is simply naïve or disingenuous. Clearly many clergy and laity (with notable exceptions) were in favour of the new services, and majorities were achieved after much debate in synod. But synodical members are notoriously unrepresentative of people in the pews, and utterly remote from the non-churchgoing population. What often occurred was similar to the forcible Catholicization found in some parishes. It involved the imposition of clerical wishes on bewildered congregations (who had hardly become familiar with one new rite before the next one appeared) by devices familiar to those who have ever been involved in church politics, and well described by Roger Homan.[47] The most recent liturgical revision culminated in Rite A and Rite B of The Alternative Service Book. This, while praised by many, has also been seen as an essentially political product, the outcome of bargaining in committee, synod and parish, which has alienated some people from the Church altogether.

Of course, any change is likely to alienate some people. But it is certainly the case that the language of Rite A in particular has been much criticized, not merely by ecclesiastical backwoodsmen, and that the music associated with this rite is widely found to be virtually unsingable. Moreover some aspects of change in the liturgy are arguably founded on a mistaken premise: that religion is a primarily cognitive activity, that it is necessary for members of congregations to understand and think about all that is said within a service. Of course, this is not possible – the average person's attention span simply cannot cope with such demands – and in any case, as Anglican Catholics traditionally understood, there are other ways of knowing than the purely cognitive – intuition and participation for example. Experience sometimes conveys what mere words cannot.

However, while the Eucharist is now the main service in most Anglican churches, its content and psychological impact have been so altered that in many cases the compelling atmosphere of Catholic worship is no longer present. What remains is what has sometimes derogatorily been called 'Protestantism in chasubles': a touch of colour to brighten up Sunday mornings. The awe, majesty, liminality and transcendence which the early Anglo-Catholics recovered are not found in many Parish Communions or Sung Eucharists. The experience of worship is thereby impoverished.

One can understand Alan Wilkinson's claim that anyone with a Catholic sensibility 'will continue to lament the failure of the Church of England with its emphasis on good taste and culture (epitomized by the upper class ethos of most English cathedrals) to produce the kind of "vulgar" Christianity which used to be found in the Anglo-Catholic slum parish, the dissenting chapels and Merseyside Roman Catholicism. Do not the Stations of the Cross, the rosary, clouds of incense, votive candles, Benediction and being splashed with buckets of holy water stand for something in religion which the Liturgical Commission will never comprehend?'[48] Even to an outsider there is a clear difference between the atmosphere produced by a restrained Parish Communion, with vestments, two acolytes but never any incense, and an atmosphere of resolute good will; and the ritualized passion of High Mass or Benediction. They belong to different orders of meaning: on the one hand a restrained rationalist religion, on the other a quest for mystery, a consciously-dramatized but no less real enchantment.

A central conclusion of this study is that recent British religious history is best understood as a battle between 'secularizing' and 'counter-secularizing' forces, a struggle between processes of 'rationalization' and 'disenchantment' on the one side, and 'de-rationalization' and 're-enchantment' on the other, to employ Weber's terminology. It is another irony of the movement's history that we see *within* Anglo-Catholicism itself a recapitulation of the world-wide Weberian struggle between the forces of rationalization and disenchantment and their opposites. The outcome of the conflict between the opposed forces is by no means certain. Indeed it is part of a much larger process of interaction between different 'faiths' which has been going on for centuries and is likely to continue into the foreseeable future.

5

Parishes and Priests

He had a mixture of dignity and equality that I had never before seen in the Anglican community. He came down amongst the congregation and told us, in a matter-of-fact and non-parsonical voice, what we were to do and what he proposed to do. He had none of the almost apologetic air common among the clergy in this century. He did not need to assume authority or intone his words to make them sound special or sacred. He spoke with unassumed authority, for he spoke as a priest.

Kingsley Martin describing Conrad Noel

The priest's role

It is a commonplace that Anglican Catholicism has been a predominantly clerical movement. The clergy began it, developed it and sustain it. Indeed one author goes so far as to suggest that it was mainly a strategy for the defence of the clerical profession. It was 'almost entirely a movement of the ordinary clergy, not of the episcopacy or laity; and, apart from any question of its spiritual appeal, it is obvious that it met a peculiar professional need of the Anglican clergy at this time'.[1] As the advantages which they enjoyed in relation to dissenting clergy were removed by legislative change in the early nineteenth century, 'unless Anglicanism developed some convincing doctrinal difference, its clergy would have difficulty in maintaining any exclusive professional position. Here the new movement came directly to their aid. By placing again in the foreground salvation through grace, grace received through sacraments, and sacraments only valid if administered by episcopally ordained clergy, it supplied exactly what the profession needed. Hence it is not surprising that, though the bishops were cold to it and the laity, as a rule, fiercely hostile, the rank and file of the clergy, including many of the ablest, came round to it more and more.'[2] This judgement exaggerates

69

both clergy involvement and the opposition of bishops and laity, but it has a grain of truth.

A similar argument regarding Free Church clergy today has been advanced by Bryan Wilson. Speaking of the problems faced by 'the clerical class', he observes that 'liturgical specialization in the new development of sacramentalism, becomes the basis of the new claim not only to authority, but also to status, with the added advantage of the weight of tradition behind it'. As they lose their social functions, clerics tend to emphasize their special expertise as custodians of religious values. '. . . precisely as clerics have lost the moral, social and pastoral aspects of their former role, so we can understand why there has tended to be a greater stress on their distinctive liturgical competence.' The cleric who has lost ground to 'experts' in social, moral and educational matters 'has obviously needed the reassurance of a special area which no other profession was likely to appropriate in the light of more modern knowledge. Thus the most ancient function of all, and the one which cannot be technologized or modernized, becomes the one to which clerical professionals return.'[3]

The Catholic movement attempted to transform the traditional role of the parson into that of the priest, possessed of a religious authority and power handed down from Jesus Christ via the apostolic succession. The origins of this type can be traced back to the middle of the nineteenth century, and the emergence of ecclesiastical pressure groups such as the Society of the Holy Cross (known as SSC from its Latin title *Societas Sanctae Crucis*), founded in February 1855.

'The chief end of SSC was to build up the priestly character. It dealt with such matters as early rising, Mass, prayer, self-examination, regular confession, intercession and retreat. It was aware that the church needed indeed able men – organizers, social, controversial – but beyond all, what she needed most was an order of men who cultivated the inner life – "full of eyes within" – those who were "set apart" (sanctified). And so the Society fostered the ecclesiastical spirit; not indeed the unreal, so often mistaken for it of a stiffness towards laymen and the things of the world, but the desire in the soul of the priest to live up to his vocation, not avoiding what interested laymen, but always bearing in mind the recollection of his priesthood and its eternal character.'[4]

The Catholic movement has produced a number of groups such as SSC: predominantly clerical and relatively small in numbers. Others in this category are the Catholic League, the

Sodality of the Precious Blood, the League of Anglican Loyalists, and Ecclesia. Small though such groups may be, historically they had a significance beyond their numbers as a focus of opposition to attempts to limit the Catholic advance. Moreover, their concentration upon the role of the priest as central to the success of the movement has two aspects worth noting. Firstly, they were clearly right up to a point in treating the priest's role as so important; arguably the movement could not have succeeded as it did without a strong leadership dispersed throughout the country. But the nature of the movement was also affected thereby: it became clericalized and authoritarian, and there were only limited attempts until recent times to build up the role of the laity. In many parishes it was very much a case of 'father knows best', with laity playing a subordinate and restricted role. This was also a factor leading to congregationalism.

However, groups such as SSC undoubtedly gave rise to a priestly ideology which was a significant source of strength for clergy in the conflicts which arose in the second half of the nineteenth century. Among its leaders were Lowder, Mackonochie, Carter, Nihill, Ommanney, Baverstock and Reginald Kingdom, all famous as pioneers of Catholicism at the parish level, and a considerable number of prominent Catholic priests have been associated with it at some time. The priest's role was sharply defined: as a man under discipline, the agent of divine power in a particular place, he saw himself as entrusted with a responsibility which he must defend against the opposition of rioting mobs, Protestant hecklers, dissident laity and hostile or indifferent bishops. His responsibility was not directly to the Church of England or to those which it had placed in authority over him, but to a broader conception of Catholic authority, inherent in that Church but not always recognized or acted upon.

'The English Provinces claimed to be both National and an integral part of the One Catholic Church of Christ. While the former claim gave them the limited liberty of a National Church, the latter claim bound them to the obedience due to the whole Church. The constitution, continuity, canons and Prayer Book of the English Church revealed this to be her mind. The bishops meant by the spirit, or mind, of the Church, their own minds and, in subjection to the State, seemed to think that by the "greater price" of the Erastian bonds, they had "obtained the freedom" of ignoring Catholic claims. The obedience they asked for was a phantom one, which faded

into thin air when measured by the standards of the Ordination Vows, or the Canonical Obedience which a priest has to
render to his bishop. Obedience to their demands would have
meant disobedience both to the Catholic Church and to the
historical interpretation of the Prayer Book, and to the
Church's true mind.'[5] The ritualistic strife which began in the
1840s was founded on such ideological points.

Bishops and priests

The position of the bishops, and their relations to their
turbulent priests, were varied and inconsistent. Broadly they
concerned themselves with the maintenance of church order,
but this had a changing interpretation as Catholic norms of
worship and doctrine became progressively institutionalized
through legal legitimation, clerical defiance and lay acceptance. In successive periods they opposed the 'Six Points' of
ritual; they fought a battle against incense in the years 1890-
1920; and in the period after the first World War they
attempted to restrict Benediction and the reservation of the
Blessed Sacrament.

In all these cases the episcopal side lost – partly because of
the ineffective sanctions which it could bring to bear, partly
because of the sympathy felt by many bishops for the pastoral
endeavours of the Catholic clergy. A number of bishops were
profoundly influenced by Tractarian ideals, and one of them,
King of Lincoln, was himself prosecuted for ritual offences
before the Archbishop of Canterbury's court in 1890. Many of
the younger Tractarian leaders were eventually to become
bishops, for example, Moberly, Wilberforce, Woodford, King,
Wilkinson, Stubbs, Talbot[6], and in a later generation, Gore,
Frere and Underhill. (Others achieved influential positions in
church and academic life, among them Bright, Liddon, Church,
Mozley, and Scott Holland.) They did not necessarily favour
'extremism'; missionary bishops like Frank Weston might have
such tendencies, but others were more like Francis Underhill,
who moderated his ideas somewhat in the twenty years
between his time as incumbent of St Alban's, Birmingham and
his consecration as Bishop of Bath and Wells in 1937. But, at
least, bishops who had been ritualists had some understanding
of, and affinity with, that school of thought.

Few bishops were successful in controlling ritual excesses.
An individual priest might be disciplined from time to time,
but policies such as the attempt to get general acceptance of a

prescribed limit to churchmanship, as by Bell of Chichester in
the 1930s[7] and attacks on the practice of reservation, as by
Barnes of Birmingham[8] similarly achieved limited and short-
lived success. In the postwar period from 1945 onwards, there
have been occasional cases where individual incumbents have
run foul of their bishops, for example at Carshalton[9] or at
Castletown.[10] But, in general, the present position seems to be
that, within very broad limits, influenced largely by the extent
of lay opposition in the parish, Catholic clergy are allowed by
their bishop to follow their own inclinations with regard to
ceremonial.

The bishop occupied a central symbolic role in the Catholic
frame of reference. It was he who made a man priest through
the rite of ordination, which was a public demonstration of
the reality of the apostolic succession, a conception which had
so preoccupied Catholics from the time of the Tracts onwards,
since it was a fundamental component of their identity as
Catholic priests. In ordination the priests believed that he
received the power to carry out sacramental functions, princi-
pally the celebration of 'the miracle of the mass' by which
Christ is made present in the bread and wine of the Eucharist.
Yet the bishop who ordained him might have a quite different
understanding of the ordination ceremony. Thorold, Bishop of
Winchester, always declared in public before ordaining his
candidates that he had no intention of making them sacrificing
priests, but only ministers of the gospel.[11] At an ordination
retreat in 1920, Hensley Henson, Bishop of Durham, delivered
a charge on the subject of lawlessness in the Church of
England which was a virulent attack on the 'tragic priests' who
ritualize the 'simple service of the Lord's Supper' and turn it
into the Roman Mass. He saw disaster ahead, as the ritualizers
captured the Church while destroying it in the process.[12]

The problem which this presented for the aspiring Catholic
priest was how to explain satisfactorily the basis of his own
belief. How could he be ordained as a sacrificing priest by a
bishop who explicitly denied any intention of making him
one? The problem was similar to that which exists when a
non-catholic Anglican celebrates the Eucharist believing it to
be no more than a memorial of the Last Supper, or a simple
fellowship meal, and certainly rejecting any notion of the
sacrifice of the Mass. The problems were analogous: they
raised the question of the relevance of intention. Thus the
same solution was possible in both cases: opening up a gap
between the officiant's intention and the efficacy of the action.

It was claimed that the rite is valid regardless of the celebrant's intention, provided that it is correctly performed.

An ideal type

To anyone who has known Anglo-Catholic priests in all their diversity, the idea of producing generalizations about their role will seem ludicrous. Their individualism was one of the weaknesses of the movement: while proclaiming the virtues of the corporate and the objective, many Catholic clergy devoted their lives to the practice of the unique and the subjective, their own version of the meaning of Catholicism. In Colin Stephenson's words, 'Anglo-Catholic clergy all had their tiny Vatican of infallible "do's and don'ts" which they would maintain in spite of any other authority'.[13]

At this point it would seem appropriate at least to refer to the endless fund of stories available to illustrate their quirks. Father Wagner of Brighton, for example, spent a vast fortune on churchbuilding, from the enormous barn of St Bartholomew's, allegedly built on the proportions of the Ark, to the subterranean Church of the Resurrection which was very damp and was soon turned into a refrigerated meat store. His father, the Vicar of Brighton, seeing the family fortune being poured away, preached from the text: 'Lord have mercy on my son, for he is a lunatic'.[14] Father William Lowndes 'had his own private oratory, and an authentic relic of Saint Anthony of Padua. He always said Mass in Latin, using the Roman rite, and he followed the Pope in everything, except on the validity or otherwise of Anglican Orders, on which matter the gift of Papal infallibility had seemingly gone wrong. Father Lowndes had come to the conclusion that the Book of Common Prayer was inspired by the Devil, and had sworn never to take part in a Prayer Book service. He seemed hardly the right man for Upminster. . . .'[15] Father Percy Maryon-Wilson, who believed that priests should be celibate, behaved as if priests' wives were not there, wearing a beatific smile while looking right through them, so that they thought him either deaf or absent-minded. Father Bristowe of Bagborough, who held similar views, went so far as to try and persuade clergy-wives to leave their husbands and boasted as a virtue of the separations he had caused.[16] No doubt some such stories are apocryphal, but they give a sense of how Anglo-Catholics liked to see their priests – i.e. as 'characters'.

The traditional priest was an authoritarian paternalist. There were at least three reasons for this. Firstly, it was generally expected of parsons in nineteenth and early twentieth century England, and the priest was likely to adopt such attitudes as part of his occupational culture. Even those slum clergy in the ritualist churches of the large towns who espoused an ecclesiastical form of socialism, and hence might have been expected to be more democratically inclined, exhibited features which have led to a recent description of them as 'squires in the East End'.[17] Secondly, the priest's high conception of his calling encouraged a certain distance from his flock; he was a man set apart to celebrate the Holy Mysteries and to teach and lead his people. The fact that SSC priests were advised not to be too 'stiff' with their people suggests that some of them were so inclined. Thirdly, the priest was a religious deviant, innovating in parishes of low catholicity, and maintaining or enhancing churchmanship in established Catholic parishes. This placed upon him the additional responsibility of leadership in the vanguard of the movement for the conversion of England to 'the Faith of our Fathers'.

Such a self-image could generate social distance in relations with parishioners, which was enhanced by the distinctive symbolic dress of biretta, cassock and cloak worn for everyday duties around the parish. Priests became known, sometimes at their own urging, as 'Father'. Considerable social differences often existed between the overwhelmingly middle class clergy and many of their lower status flock (though there was also a significant element of affluent middle class laity who would meet the costs of ritual innovation; Lord Halifax, Samuel Gurney, Sir Hubert Miller, Sir William Milner and Athelstan Riley for example). Priests also attracted sometimes unwelcome attention from two of the stereotypical lay followers of the movements – ardent young men and lonely middle-aged ladies – and in such cases social distance could be an effective protection.

Commitment to celibacy by a significant minority of priests also added to the distinctive character of the role. This was linked in some cases to a homosexual orientation, indications of which were apparent from the Tractarian period onward. Some of the leaders such as Newman, Froude and Faber contracted fervent masculine friendships.[18] As Edward Norman notes, Tractarianism often seemed to be associated with effeminacy.[19] It was said that Cuddesdon curates were 'unmanly'; Bishop Wilberforce spoke of their want of 'vigour

... virility ... and vitality'. When Edward King, later bishop of Lincoln, was principal, close and sentimental personal relationships developed rapidly in the college. King himself was the subject of rumours in relation to Stephen, the son of Prime Minister Gladstone, which led to gossip about his chances of preferment.[20] Either effeminacy or homosexuality is implied in many comments on Anglo-Catholics, especially the clergy. Rayner Heppenstall regarded Christians of the Anglo-Catholic persuasion as constituting a kind of intellectual third sex. Fr Eric Cheetham, Vicar of St Stephen's, Gloucester Road in the time of T. S. Eliot, 'like many Anglo-Catholic priests . . . seemed not altogether masculine. A pastime to which he was seriously addicted was dressmaking.'[21] And the small boys who take part either as choristers or servers in Anglo-Catholic services have sometimes been the subject of attentions from male admirers.[22] Harry Williams' book gives a vivid picture of the homosexual element to be found among some Catholics; and also a moving account of his attempts to cope with his own homosexual orientation.

At the same time an undoubted charisma resulted from the priest's apartness, whatever its basis, and from the social concern with which many were associated. The history of the Catholic movement is studded with the names of heroes of the faith – Lowder, Wainwright, Mackonochie, Dolling, Stanton and others – and with legends of their work among the poor in slum parishes. This charismatic element was also enhanced by the evident self-sacrifice which such men displayed, both in social action and in the abandonment of hope of career advancement. A number of priests went to Catholic parishes knowing that by their actions they might be committed to a lifetime as a curate in the same church, possibly under discipline from their own bishops (which meant, that they were effectively cut off from diocesan life along with their parishioners), and prevented from officiating in other dioceses by episcopal inhibition.

Isolation of this sort had certain advantages, while also encouraging the introverted congregationalism with which Anglican Catholicism is sometimes associated. The priest was able, within the contraints set by parishioners' support, Protestant harassment and episcopal intervention, to develop parish and churchmanship as he chose. A number of clergy had private incomes which they were more than ready to devote to the futherance of the Catholic cause, and they used these to transform their churches into eclectic replicas of continental Roman Catholicism, adorned with statues, candles, confessionals and tabernacles, and to ensure that the liturgy was performed with maximum elaboration and splendour. Where personal income was not available, expenses might be met by affluent lay enthusiasts, or the funds of religious pressure groups such as the Church Union, the Catholic League, the Confraternity of the Blessed Sacrament or the Guild of All Souls.

Another advantage derived from the physical isolation of parishes, either in the remote countryside or in urban villages. Here social life might be focused on the church to a greater extent than in more accessible areas, since there were few alternative attractions, and forms of Catholic community could become established. The organization of leisure activities for both children and adults was seen as being good in itself. At the lowest level it provided an alternative to the public house. More positively, it represented a conception of the role of church or chapel wider than that of simply a place of worship or 'soul-saving' agency: in Fr Wainwright's terms, the parish church as focus of the parochial 'family' and the place for confessions and processions, for dancing and for cricket, each at its due time; in Fr Dolling's terms, 'the chief centre for social righteousness to the whole district', providing for 'man– body, soul and spirit . . . treated as a whole'. Stewart Headlam saw it as 'the best and the largest secular society'. Such social ventures were often very successful in the nineteenth century, but they achieved few conversions, and while boys' clubs continued to flourish, those for men were eventually killed off by competition from the wireless, the cinema and the dog track.[23]

In a few cases funds were employed to buy houses and cottages for the use of Catholics drawn from further afield by the attraction of 'full Catholic privileges'. Thus a remote village church like Throwleigh in Devon could boast in the mid-1940s a daily mass attendance of 12; 9,000 church attendances and 5,000 communions a year; weekly Holy Hour and Benediction, and many penitents.[24]

There were disadvantages in such isolation. Firstly it encouraged priestly individualism: church and parish were the property of one dominant individual, who moulded them according to his own views, drawing selectively from the available apparatus of Catholicism, sometimes in a highly eccentric fashion. Secondly there was the parochialism and congregationalism which weakened the wider movement. Its solidarity, and potential for united action was reduced due to the inability of some priests to co-operate with each other, which was the outcome not only of personal idiosyncrasy but also of the ideological divisions within the movement.

The priest today

Today the typical Catholic priest's role is very different from that of the classical period. Firstly, he is part of a movement manifestly in decline and undergoing radical change. The Catholic pressure groups are no longer triumphalist, but uncertainly seeking their way in a very different world from that of the 1930s. Congregations have fallen rapidly, and in some cases are virtually non-existent. In many places the daily Mass is a thing of the past. Remote country churches can be found where the Sunday Sung Mass attracts a congregation of half a dozen, the statues are dusty, the sanctuary lamps unpolished and unlit, and the tabernacle empty. A number of well-known churches were destroyed by wartime bombing and have not been rebuilt, and programmes of pastoral reorganization, sometimes interpreted as anti-catholic in intention, have closed others. The Parish Communion has replaced High Mass in some places with a subsequent decline in traditional churchmanship. Many of the Catholic societies have experienced a reduction in membership and complain about lack of support for their festivals. Their influence on the priest's self-image is now more as a moribund cult than as a vigorous and thriving movement.

Two priestly types exemplify current problems of the Catholic party. Firstly there is a continuing traditional type, small in numbers and carrying on an uphill struggle to maintain full ritual and doctrine. This group is under pressure, not only from the sources already mentioned, but also from the generation gap which exists between them and the younger clergy who act as their curates. A clerical version of inter-generational conflict can arise, in which a decline which is basically structural in origin can be attributed for the purposes of argument either to a loss of Catholic fullness and discipline, or to the fruitless attempt to maintain old-fashioned ways. The older group is often reluctant to acknowledge the extent of decline, and is critical of open discussion as 'the washing of dirty linen in public'.[25]

The second type is that of the newer Catholic clergy, particularly those ordained since the 1950s. Priestly charisma and authoritarianism are no longer available. Some clergy see home visiting as a waste of time, and thus lose the opportunity to influence parishioners at the personal level. Any possibility of building up traditional forms of authority or charismatic influence is hampered by the mobility of both clergy and laity. Priests, especially curates, tend to move frequently, partly because of changing patterns of diocesan need, partly in search of wider responsibilities or progress up the emerging bureaucratic hierarchies, and also because of a diminishing desire for commitment to one parish as a vocation for life. This contrasts sharply with the older pattern of long incumbencies, extreme examples of which are found in the parish of Throwleigh, already mentioned, which had only three Rectors in the first sixty years of this century, Hinton Martel in Dorset which had four, or Bridgerule in Devon, where Frank Hawker Kingdon was Vicar for seventy years. Laity also move more frequently than previously, with the consequence that parish traditions are harder to sustain, as is any legitimation of the priest's authority on a traditional basis. For both these reasons the older authoritarian paternalism is now unusual.

Priests are brought closer to their laity by the increasing recruitment of clergy from lower social strata than before. The biretta is seldom worn, and the cassock less frequently outside the church. Clerical attitudes to the decline of authority in the old sense are frequently ambivalent: while formally rejecting claims to traditional authority, some clergy behave in an authoritarian fashion and display irritation at 'sheep who will not be led'. Conflict with parishioners is a result. This seems to be particularly true of Catholic clergy.[26] It exacerbates for Catholics the general feeling of loneliness and isolation which many clergy of all persuasions experience due to the general insecurities of the clerical role.[27]

A strong ideology of the traditional sort might be an effective support in such circumstances, but recently ordained Catholic clergy appear to be peculiarly vulnerable to the ideas of current liberal theology.[28] Moreover, the growth of the Parish Communion has assisted a process of ideological dilution through which moderate Catholic ritual is now associated with a variety of theological orientations. Thus Catholic externals are no longer a guarantee of Catholic orthodoxy, and are frequently unaccompanied by a stress on Catholic doctrine or discipline.

A pattern has been observed in a number of parishes where the priest, faced with a congregation of mixed traditions – itself a reflection of changes in social structure and the growth of mobility in church congregations – attempts to conciliate non-catholics by reducing the 'fullness' of Catholicism. For example, there may be changes of terminology – what was previously 'the Mass' is now referred to as 'the Eucharist' or 'the Parish Communion'. Writers frequently claim that 'the name does not matter'. While this is no doubt theologically correct it is sociologically insensitive, and neglects the symbolic significance of language. 'Mass' carries a rich charge of historical meaning, both in relation to the pre-Reformation Church and to the Catholic revival; its replacement symbolizes a small step away from Catholic tradition for reasons which are basically political.

Some other changes have a similar significance. The use of incense is ended or reduced; devotions such as Benediction and Holy Hour cease or are relegated to a weekday evening; the meetings of devotional societies such as the Confraternity of the Blessed Sacrament or the Society of our Lady of Walsingham are focused around the Eucharist rather than Benediction; the Angelus and the Rosary are no longer said. All these changes can be justified theologically and pastorally, or even on the commonsense ground that there is no reason why Catholicism should be tied to a particular set of liturgical expressions so long as the truths of the faith are maintained. But this is slightly disingenuous: those truths were embodied in the abandoned practices, and they inevitably suffer in the minds of those familiar with their meaning. Catholic laity may accept the changes for worthy reasons, but their own confidence can suffer a blow which may affect their practice. A pattern of slow erosion is noticeable, where changes made for such reasons do not bring about an improvement in non-catholic attendence or involvement, but do weaken Catholic adherence. Traditional demands for the maintenance of 'the full faith' often have greater sociological force than modern attempts to dilute it.

So far as the priest is concerned, there appears to be not merely a change of direction but a loss of confidence. In the triumphalist period priests were clear that their task was to spread the full faith, and that meant fighting for incense, Benediction and devotion to our Lady against many sources of opposition. In fifty years that commitment has been greatly attenuated. Some Anglican Catholics are now themselves carrying out the protestantization of the faith which their forefathers fought against so hard, and display considerable insensitivity to the social function of symbols.

Thus the irony of the Catholic movement's present situation reappears. Though virtually all the innovations for which earlier generations of Catholics fought are now generally possible, in practice they are desired less and less by many clergy. A simpler liturgy, the dismantling of shrines and altars, the abandonment of traditional services, less emphasis on confession or the keeping of a rule of life, are now features of a Catholic group which stresses the communitarian aspects of the Eucharist rather than its mystery, and which prefers Rite A to the English Missal or even the Missa Normativa.

Changes of this kind facilitate ecumenism (together with the increasing ritualism in nonconformity[29] and the changes in post-conciliar Roman Catholicism) but they provide fewer structural or ideological supports for the distinctive vocation of the priest. Catholics are caught up in the debate about the meaning of the ministry in a secular society as much as any other group; indeed their predecessors helped begin it with their contribution to the liberal Catholicism of the nineteenth century.

Those with a traditional bias find themselves in a quandry. Not only is the Church of England changing, but so too is Rome, the previous refuge for insecure Anglo-Catholic clergy. In the post-Vatican 2 period it has encompassed so much change that many see little difference between the Roman and Anglican versions of Catholicism, not merely in externals but to an increasing extent in doctrine, as the joint body ARCIC pursues its deliberations on doctrinal issues.[30] In such a situation the one unwavering source of traditional rectitude is the Orthodox Church, and this has experienced an increase in conversions from Anglicanism (not only of clergy) in recent years. In a changing world the numinous power of the Orthodox liturgy can provide an increasingly attractive anchor, when both Canterbury and Rome seem to be slipping their moorings.

There is a decline in vocations to the priesthood; some Catholic colleges have closed. Some younger clergy devote much of their time to community welfare work, and involvement in movements like Oxfam and Shelter, which take the place in parish life of devotional societies such as the Confraternity of the Blessed Sacrament or the Society of Mary. Social involvement is of course part of the Catholic tradition, but while historically this sprang directly from an incarnational theology underpinned by a strong Catholic spirituality, the order of priorities is reversed for many of the present generation, or the social commitment lacks any such base. When this is so, full time social work, and even sociology itself, can provide an attractive alternative to the priesthood for men with social commitment who are critical of church structures and tradition. This sort of secularization is less likely, however, where priests have a clear understanding of the Catholic vision, a disciplined spiritual life and a realistic understanding of what is possible in today's world.

6

The Religious Orders

Community life is a persistent characteristic of Christendom. This is natural, since Christianity is founded in Sacrifice, the greatest, most awful sacrifice ever conceived, and Monasticism is a noble expression of the sacrificial spirit. A community wholly dedicated to the service of Religion has in its very nature capacities for completer renunciation and self-surrender to the one undivided aim than can be found elsewhere.

W. J. Sparrow Simpson

Introduction

The urge to separate oneself from the world may be felt only by a minority, but it seems to be a recurrent aspect of human experience, mainly occurring within a religious context which both legitimates and institutionalizes it. As with St Francis[1] it is a way of total commitment to a supernaturally-oriented way of life, a form of spiritual perfectionism. It provides society with a means of symbolic demonstration of the truths of the faith, a public affirmation of the primacy of spiritual values, and a channel by means of which the disruptive effects of spiritual perfectionism may be controlled.

For a period of three hundred years such a separation was not officially recognized within the Church of England; when it reappeared it became the focus of contention and riot. For Anglican Catholics the reappearance of orders within the English Church was both a means to types of experience possible only for religious virtuosi, and a sign that the Church was truly as Catholic as it claimed.

There are other implications of the emergence of Anglican religious orders. Again the anti-modernism theme appears: Catholics, as Graham Davies notes, shared in the general nostalgia of the time for a mythical golden age, a lost rural paradise characterized by hierarchy and paternalism.[2] Similarly

John Kent has argued that the attempt to revive monasticism was grounded in opposition to industrialization and its social consequences, and offered an alternative social ideal which was its exact opposite.[3]

Anglican Catholics seeking to restore Catholic doctrine and practice to the Church of England can be seen as like customers in a restaurant, confronted with a menu on which all the dishes are attractive, and possible if one is following a 'Catholic' diet. The question which arises is, 'What shall we have, and in what order?' Choice is influenced by the hierarchy of values stated in, or implied by, the ideology. The Mass is at the heart of Catholicism and therefore has to be given a high priority, which is in turn related to the status and authority of the ministers of the sacrament. So clearly the priesthood, the doctrine of the apostolic succession, and eucharistic theology are the central issues to be established first. After that the choices are not so clear and other factors intervene. Among these may be the affective pull of certain images – the attraction of following as closely as possible in the footsteps of Christ, an icon of total commitment, total self-giving. Clarke sees monasticism as exemplifying the spirit of the Catholic movement: 'at once a call to holiness and a return to antiquity . . . it represented the desire of the individual to devote himself, or herself, wholly to the immediate service of God, and to follow the example of the Lord . . . it shows, to say the least, a passionate desire for holiness. It was a return to antiquity because the idea of monasticism is as old as the New Testament. Our Lord blessed those who remained unmarried for the kingdom of heaven's sake, and counselled a young man to part with his possessions and follow Him.'[4] And as Sparrow Simpson remarks, aware of the importance of communal support in such aims, 'The individual acquires immense access of strength from the corporate spirit of his Order'. Moreover, the Catholic movement as a whole has benefited: 'The cause of Religion is promoted not only in the ordinary domestic way. It is not only the Creeds of Christendom and the Liturgies, it is also the Monastic orders which link the Church of today with the Church of the centuries.'[5]

The choices of both individuals and groups will also be conditioned by their social position and how this affects, for example, the availability of economic resources to support new ventures; and by the alternative choices available to particular sections of the population, such as women. Both these factors were of importance in the revival of Anglican religious orders. At the most mundane level, convent buildings had to be paid for, and a woman might only decide to enter an order if alternative careers were limited.[6]

But clearly also for some Anglican Catholics the presence of religious orders is an essential feature of Catholicism, not merely one of a number of possibilities. Sparrow Simpson states that, 'Wherever Catholicism prevails Monasticism appears'.[7] Ollard claims that 'Wherever the Catholic Church is planted certain fruits grow. You always find the Creeds, you always find the Canon of Holy Scripture, you always find the threefold ministry descending from the Apostles, you always find the sacraments . . . But also, at least since St Anthony in the third century . . . you find the religious life in the technical sense, i.e. men and women, singly or in communities, devoting themselves to the service of God, and living apart from the world under a rule.'[8] And that presence can be seen either as evidence of divine power at work in the Church, or as a public demonstration that the Church is truly Catholic – in other words, orders may be necessary as part of the process by which Catholicism is socially constructed. A properly Catholic Church must have monks and nuns, even recluses and hermits. The first is a theological interpretation, the second is socio-logical; and they are not necessarily incompatible. Motives are often mixed and not always conscious.

We can certainly find fragmentary evidence that the second position was held by some nineteenth century Anglicans. Father Ignatius of Llanthony, the eccentric founder of an early Anglican Benedictine order, explicitly argued that monasteries are one of the chief features of the Catholic religion. If the Church of England does not possess them at present because of the capricious actions of a past monarch, it is necessary that they should be restored as a way of showing that the Church is indeed Catholic. In his thespian way, Ignatius was conscious of what audiences expected, and of the props necessary to play a part properly. In 1863, he and two companions set up a monastery in part of the rectory at Claydon in Suffolk, where the Rector said Mass for them every morning and they recited the Breviary (which Ignatius had to translate since he was the only one who knew Latin). He was also the organist and musical arranger, borrowing from various classical sources. In his later foundation at Llanthony in the Black Mountains he employed a spectacular form of penance: every day a brother was led into choir with a rope round his neck, the community spat at him and walked over him while he lay prostrate; he was then obliged to beg for his food until someone else took over the role next day. Ignatius was also splendidly anti-intellectual: 'We never allow ourselves to think', he wrote, 'It is all decided for us'.[9]

Religious orders within the Church of England have always been relatively small in numbers, especially by comparison with the Roman Catholic Church. Women have always greatly outnumbered men, perhaps because of the opportunities already available for men in the ordained ministry. There was a great deal of instability in the early years, a common feature of utopian communities generally.[10] Detailed information, which does not however cover the recent period, is readily found in Peter F. Anson's magisterial account.[11] This lists 34 male orders founded in Great Britain between 1842 and 1961, of which 19 had become extinct and 3 had joined the Church of Rome. Between 1845 and 1952, 118 female orders were founded; 60 of these were extinct by 1964 and 1 had joined the Church of Rome.

In the century after 1833 the orders grew rapidly. By 1878, in the province of Canterbury alone there were nearly 700 sisters, novices and postulants. Taking into account the sisters in the Province of York, and the much smaller numbers of brothers, a very considerable growth had occurred within a space of 45 years. By 1940 there were about 1,400 women and 150 men in religious orders throughout the Anglican communion.[12] As a matter of interest the number of women was approximately double that in orders at the time of the dissolution of the monasteries.[13]

By 1963 the numbers were even higher: 1,801 women and 275 men in the provinces of Canterbury and York. There had been 'a good half-century of steady growth'.[14] It is worth noting that in 1963 there were 6.5 women religious within Anglicanism for every male, but only 3.2 within Roman Catholicism. The predominance of females within Anglican Catholicism is as apparent here as elsewhere. By the 1980s a dramatic fall had occurred among women, and a smaller one among male religious who were priests: 37.5 per cent and 10.8 per cent respectively. The latter figure was exactly offset by an increase in lay monks, so that the total remained unchanged from that of 22 years before. Thus there were still 275 men (1985) but only 1,126 women (1984 – the latest year available at the time of writing), a female/male ratio of 4.1 to 1. The significance of these figures is discussed later.

The beginning of Anglican orders

The rationale for the revival of religious orders was the need
for a practical response to the nursing of the poor. In 1826 the
Revd A. R. Dallas, curate of Wooburn in Buckinghamshire, who
had served in the Peninsula War where he had seen the work
done by religious orders, wrote a pamphlet entitled *Protestant
Sisters of Charity*, addressed to the Bishop of London and
advocating the formation of societies akin to the Sisters of
Charity of St Vincent de Paul. This idea was taken up by a
prominent philanthropist, Dr Gooch, who wrote articles in
Blackwoods and the *London Medical Gazette*, in which he
drew attention to the great suffering of the rural poor due to
the lack of adequate medical attention. Such attendants as
were found were motivated, he wrote perceptively, by 'scientific zeal, by mere natural humanity, or by mercenary motives;
but these cannot be trusted for steady attention – the one
subsides with the solution of a question, the other hardens
by habit, the last requires jealous inspection – we want
an actuating motive of a more steady and enduring nature,
which requires neither curiosity, nor emotion, nor avarice to
keep it alive, which still burns in the most tranquil states of
mind, and out of reach of human inspection, and this motive
is religion. . . .' A carefully selected group of women should be
recruited, given a practical medical education, and set to
work in country parishes on the same lines as Catholic Sisters
of Charity. A correspondence developed in which one of the
participants was the Quaker Elizabeth Fry, who began to put
such ideas into effect in Whitechapel.[15]
   The most influential contributor to the debate was Robert
Southey, who wrote a well-known and much-quoted appeal for
the formation of sisterhoods. 'Why, then, have you no
Beguines, no Sisters of Charity? Why in the most needful, the
most merciful form that charity can take have you not followed
the example of the French and the Netherlands? No Vincent
de Paul has been heard in your pulpits: no Louise de Gras has
appeared among the daughters of Great Britain. Piety has
found its way into your prisons; your hospitals are imploring it
in vain; nothing is wanting in them but religious charity; and
ah, what a want is that! . . .' Significantly in view of later
conflicts, he added, 'There is nothing Romish, nothing superstitious, nothing fanatical in such associations, nothing but
what properly belongs to that *threskeia*, that religious service,

which the Apostle James, the brother of our Lord, has told us is pure and undefiled before God and the Father'.[16]

Alongside the identification of need and proposals for its solution a second factor was important: strong motivation. As Southey remarked, 'A call of this kind must not be looked for from the pulpit, at least not from the Church pulpits. To make it, there would be required a spirit of enthusiasm, which they whose duty it is to keep things in order, and within their appointed bounds, seek always to repress.' Such enthusiasm, rare in religion at the time, was supplied by the coming of the Oxford Movement. The ideal of the religious life was inherent in Tractarian belief with its stress on the norms of the primitive Church, which could be appealed to as a source of legitimacy, thus meeting accusations of Romanizing. A far more fundamental factor was the Tractarian demand for a total commitment to the divine purpose.

Behind these motives, of course, was the Romanticism which is such a fundamental part of the Catholic movement. The glamour of monasticism was evidently an influence on a number of pioneers, most spectacularly in the case of Joseph Leycester Lyne ('Father Ignatius'), who attempted the revival of the Benedictine life in the English Church, less obviously in others but present nonetheless. Romanticism generated a powerful emotional response to its images of Gothic mystery, nowhere more so than in the convents, monasteries and churches which Victorian wealth enabled to be built as a realization of the dreams of the past 'ages of faith' which Romanticism inspired.

During their early years, the sisterhoods were regarded with intense suspicion and mistrust. Only three bishops – Wilberforce of Oxford, Philpotts of Exeter and Tait of London – would give them any encouragement, and even these were firmly opposed to the taking of vows and 'habitual confession'. In their opposition to vows, oddly enough, they were more in accord with the 'mind' of the Catholic Church than the founders of the new communities, since, as Anson points out, the Holy See had allowed few communities of women to take solemn vows since the time of the French Revolution.[17]

Perhaps the emotional pull of vows was stronger in this instance than that of conformity to Rome. Certainly the call to the cloister was strong enough to justify disregard of episcopal approval where that was not forthcoming. Peter Anson remarks that many of the older sisterhoods were virtually autonomous for years, without any supervision by a bishop.[18] Just as ritual was brought under legal and executive scrutiny, so too was the religious life, and there was even a Select Committee on Conventual and Monastic Institutions which published a Report full of fascinating detail in 1870. But not until the Lambeth Conference of 1897 did the episcopate discuss religious communities, or make proposals for relating them to the authority structure of the Church.

It was in such circumstances as these that the first Anglican sisterhoods emerged. In 1841 Pusey wrote to Newman as follows: 'A young lady, who is very grateful for your teaching, is proposing today to take a vow of holy celibacy. She has difficulties and anxieties in her position. She has attended at S. Mary's since she has been in Oxford, and hopes to receive Holy Communion there to-day as part of her self-devotion. It was wished that you should know it and remember her. You will know her by her being dressed in white with an ivory cross.' This was Marian Hughes, the first woman for over three hundred years to take the vows of a nun in the English Church, though she had neither a community nor a religious superior. The private nature of her vows indicates the caution which pioneers of religious orders displayed in the climate of public hostility to Romanism. Eight years later, in 1849, she was to found the Community of the Holy and Undivided Trinity, but the first example of community life as such came from another source.

In 1845 Pusey and others founded the first English sisterhood since the Reformation. This was the Sisterhood of the Holy Cross, which took up residence at 17, Park Village West, St John's Wood, under the supervision of the Vicar of Christ Church, Albany Street, the Revd Mr Dodsworth, with Pusey as spiritual director. A Miss Langston was appointed as superior, and the community began at Easter 1845 with three resident sisters. It was modelled on the Sisters of Charity and had four aims: (i) to visit the poor in their own homes; (ii) to visit hospitals, workhouses and prisons; (iii) to feed, clothe and instruct destitute children; (iv) to assist in burying the dead. The daily life of the sisters was structured by prayer, beginning with Mattins and Lauds at 5.20 and concluding with Compline at 9.00; there were six other services during the day, and periods for private prayer and spiritual reading. Taking into account the charitable activities as well, the demands made on the women's time were considerable. There were difficulties from the outset. Among the reasons suggested for this are poor leadership by the superior; that the sisters were too old and set

in their ways to adjust to their new life; that Pusey was too
ready to grant relaxation from the rule; and that the sisters
were made too much of; they were 'spoilt', in Keble's view. The
sisters obtained favourable publicity for their work with
Florence Nightingale in the Crimea, and the order took up
work in London, but it did not flourish, and was eventually
absorbed into the Society of the Holy Trinity, whose superior,
Priscilla Lydia Sellon, was to have a great deal of influence on
the development of women's communities.

In 1848 the three types of religious life, active, enclosed and
mixed, were all revived. The Nursing Sisters of St John the
Divine adopted the active life, saying morning, noon and
evening offices rather than the canonical hours. The mixed
form was represented by an order which after a shaky start
developed into one of the strongest Anglican orders. It began
when Elizabeth Lockhart, sister of a disciple of Newman, and
three other women, adopted the religious life at Wantage,
Berks, a move encouraged and supervised by the vicar, W. J.
Butler, who wanted a teaching sisterhood to assist in his
ministry. The contrast between the active and contemplative
approaches was summed up by him in his instructions to his
community, employing the much-used contrast between
Martha and Mary. 'To serve is Martha's special work, to contemplate is Mary's. Martha provided that Mary may have leisure
to gaze. Mary could not contemplate did not Martha serve ...
the two characters form a perfect whole. Each may, neither
need, fail ... Martha may be cumbered about much serving,
Mary may sit at Christ's feet and despise her sister. Yet while
Martha serves for the love of Christ, gladly aiding Mary, while
Mary sits for the love of Christ, gladly praying for Martha, His
blessing is on each, each has a portion of the blessing of the
other ... in this present time surely Martha's work must be the
fittest preparation for Mary's.'[19] Despite problems caused by
early defections to Rome, this foundation developed into one
of the best-known Anglican sisterhoods, the Community of St
Mary the Virgin. CSMV employed the full canonical hours but
undertook various types of parish and institutional work.

By far the most ambitious scheme for sisterhoods was begun
in the west country in 1848. Henry Philpotts, Bishop of Exeter,
appealed for volunteers to work among the poor in Plymouth
and Devonport. In response, Priscilla Lydia Sellon, who had
already considered joining Pusey's Park Village Sisterhood in
London, came forward.[20] She was the daughter of a naval
Commander, who said that he had 'early trained her in the

school of obedience and duty', and she was to show that she had inherited a formidable personal authority over others. Within two years, as 'Mother Lydia', she had founded schools for sailor boys, homes for orphans, a refuge for girls, a home for old sailors and their wives, ragged schools, soup kitchens and lodging houses, in all nearly twenty charitable institutions. The Devonport Sisters became famous for their work during the cholera outbreaks of 1849 and 1853, during which they began the practice of daily Communion, the first occasion on which there had been a daily Eucharist, so far as is known, in the Church of England since the Reformation. They also attracted attention from opponents. 'They were accused, denounced, vilified from pulpit, press and platform as "Jesuits", manœuvrers with deep craft and cunning for the establishment of their impious purposes.'[21]

The bishop held an enquiry into these accusations and completely exonerated the sisters. He declared that they had 'endured more than I ever knew women to be called upon to endure', and expressed his 'most unmixed admiration' for their labours. Their numbers grew rapidly at first: eight sisters were sent out to help Florence Nightingale during the Crimean War, and by 1867 there was even a branch house in Honolulu. Amalgamation suggested further growth: the Devonport Sisters of Mercy were combined with the Park Village Sisterhood of the Holy Cross in 1856, as the Society of the Most Holy Trinity, under the spiritual direction of Pusey, who hoped that Mother Lydia might become the first Superior-General of the Anglican sisterhoods, though this was not to happen. The active work of the order was gradually discarded, and by 1876, shortly after the death of Mother Lydia, the community was mainly settled at Ascot Priory, with some welfare work in Plymouth, but with the emphasis of its activities now on the more contemplative aspects of the religious life. The early growth was not sustained; there were no new postulants to the first and third orders between 1874 and 1890, and while some came later, the Society was forced to reduce its commitments from the early 1860s onwards, eventually withdrawing from Plymouth in 1906 to concentrate at Ascot. In recent years the orphanage and convalescent home have been leased out and transformed into a residential home for the elderly.

Another major women's foundation had begun at Clewer, Berks, in 1851. Here the Rector, Revd T. T. Carter, was concerned about the conditions of the poor of his parish, especially women involved in vice. The need for a 'peniten-

tiary' to carry the work further was felt, and Mr Carter decided
this should be run by a sisterhood. The difficulties faced by the
first orders were fully apparent at Clewer. The superior,
Mother Harriet, had no knowledge of either convents abroad
or the rules of Roman Catholic communities, and was totally
dependent on Mr Carter's advice and direction. None of the
women forming the initial group had any experience of life in
a religious community. At the same time they were engaged in
training a much larger group of women living in the same
establishment. Moreover, Mr Carter himself, reflecting the
limitations in clergy training at the time, had no specialized
knowledge of theology, especially dogmatic and mystical
theology, and was self-taught in such matters in his later life. He
and Mother Harriet had to travel abroad to study the operation
of Roman communities for inspiration.[22] In the early days no
vows were taken, since Carter himself disapproved of them, and
Wilberforce would never have agreed to the foundation had
they been taken. However, 'it has always been the feeling of the
Sisters that their purpose and conviction is a lifelong dedica-
tion of themselves.'[23]

Clewer's aim was to combine the active and contemplative
forms of the religious life. Mother Harriet's attitude to the
relation between the two aspects was flexible: Carter wrote
that she saw 'devotion as (the) root power, but with readiness
to accommodate the rule of devotion to the exigencies of the
souls among whom the Sister may be set to work'. She thought
of the Community as a series of concentric circles, with the
ideal of St John the Baptist at the centre. The circles were
composed of the sisters bound together in the common life,
each having 'a revelation of the Triune Divine Life and a mani-
festation of the Mind of Christ'. For Mother Harriet the
practical and the devotional were interwoven, but the spiritual
life always came first.

Mission work was undertaken in the district, leading eventu-
ally to the foundation in 1867 of the new parish of Clewer St
Stephen, to become a Anglo-Catholic stronghold, which
demonstrates the common pattern of a more advanced cere-
monial from the outset than was found in the parish church of
St Andrew. In 1860 sisters were sent to work at St Barnabas',
Pimlico where they opened a school, an orphanage, an alms-
house and a refuge. Mission houses were set up at St Mary's,
Soho (1862), St Alban's, Holborn (1868) and All Hallows',
Southwark (1870). Work was undertaken in Devon and in
Oxford, leading to the foundation of further penitentiaries.

Growth during this period was very great, and the first overseas foundation was made in 1874. Mother Harriet retired in 1875 and died in 1883. After her death the work of expansion continued, with new houses of mercy at Great Maplestead, Essex (1892), Torquay (1892), Highgate (1900), Dartford (1901), and work in India and the United States.

A number of other well-known sisterhoods began in the 1850s and after. While space prevents discussion of their work and growth, mention should be made of the Community of All Saints (1851), the Sisters of St Margaret (1854), founded by J. M. Neale, and the Community of the Blessed Virgin Mary (1855) founded by Father Wagner as one of his many contributions to the catholicization of Brighton. An average of five new orders were established in each decade up to the end of the century.

The male orders

The revival of male orders began about the same time as Miss Hughes took her vows, with Newman's brotherhood at Littlemore, founded in 1841, whose six members led a life of 'retirement, study and prayer' centred on the Breviary. Newman denied that it was a monastery 'in anything approaching to the Romanist sense of the term', but it only lasted until Newman's secession to Rome in 1845. It was nonetheless of significance as the first male foundation since the Reformation and the most important experiment since Little Gidding. There was also a short-lived community in Leeds which worried Hook. He wrote to Pusey on 21 November 1843, 'I am uneasy about Mr Aitken. . . . He has fitted up the schoolroom adjoining his church with cells, each containing a bed and a cross; he has some young men with him who have forsaken all; his rule is very strict; he has daily Communion; they fast till four every Wednesday, when he allows himself, and themselves, meat; on Friday they fast till four and then have fish. In the meantime he, having a family residing five miles away, sleeps in his cell four times a week . . . ; his wife complains of his neglecting his six or more children.'[24] At about the same time Faber formed a similar community at Elton, Hunts, which collapsed when he also was received into the Roman Church in 1845 along with seven members of his brotherhood.

Following these failures male orders were not attempted again for some years. The Brotherhood of St James was formed at Tamworth in 1855 by the Revd Edward Steer, later Bishop of

Zanzibar, but only lasted for a short time. In 1862 Joseph Leycester Lyne ('Father Ignatius') was made curate of St Peter's Plymouth, and with the encouragement of Mother Lydia and Dr Pusey set about the revival of the Benedictine life in the Church of England.[25] Lyne was an individualist who provoked opposition throughout his life. Though a 'definite Catholic', he seems to have been very effective as an evangelistic preacher (again illustrating the combination of the two elements within Anglican Catholicism), but he also attracted hostility because of his colourful eccentricities, and as he himself remarked, had been 'pelted with mud and rotten eggs, hooted and jeered by a yelling mob, spat upon, and often in fear of life'. Eventually he began the building of a monastery at Llanthony in the Black Mountains of Wales on St Patrick's Day 1870. Since he was only a deacon, and no bishop would ordain him, there were problems from the outset, and eventually he was ordained in 1898 by an *episcopus vagans*, which effectively cut him off from the Church of England. Despite this his foundation was among the more enduring revivals, and lasted from 1863 till its amalgamation with the Caldey Benedictines in 1910. Clarke remarks of him that although he might be condemned for having put the monastic revival on the level of comic opera, other communities 'of the strictest orthodoxy and unimpeachable correctness . . . may nevertheless owe their very existence to the publicity which he gave to the religious life as a possible vocation for men'.[26] No publicity is bad publicity.

A far more sober venture was Richard Meux Benson's foundation in 1865 of the Society of St John the Evangelist, the Cowley Fathers.[27] Benson was a quiet, retiring and reserved person, who had intended to be a missionary in India until requested to be Vicar of Cowley by Bishop Wilberforce in 1850. After a meeting presided over by Pusey at All Saints', Margaret Street in 1865, Benson agreed to become the director of a male brotherhood. The first community was set up in Benson's house in Magdalen Terrace, Oxford. Its aim was prayer, study and mission work. Ultimately it was hoped to have a house in Oxford for undergraduates wishing to live under a rule, theology students, and clergy engaged in study; a chapel in London to 'address the educated classes'; foreign missions; and retreats. The day was ordered by prayer, beginning with Lauds, Prime and meditation at 6.00 and ending with Compline at 10.00. There were six further services during the day, and the practical activities undertaken were teaching and visiting.

Benson fought shy of the more spectacular manifestations of Anglican monasticism displayed by Father Ignatius. Monasticism was not a mere product of fashion but should spring from an internal call from God. Vocation must be thoroughly tested by a two-year novitiate following a three-month postulancy. No one would be fully professed under the age of thirty. Discipline would be strict and the liturgy simple. The iron church in the Iffley Road where it was celebrated was ugly, bare and uncomfortable. Benson himself appears to have had what might be called a 'negative charisma': he impressed because he was so unglamorous: thin, wiry, ascetic, shortsighted, shabby, with a harsh though hesitant voice. Ollard refers to him as 'this amazing man with a frame described as "a combination of catgut and iron", spending whole nights in prayer and writing, fasting for a whole day even when he was over ninety. Crippled with rheumatism, deaf, and almost blind, "his mental powers were scarcely impaired and his spiritual powers in no way lessened" . . . as you get the last vision of that old man of nearly ninety-one, hoping soon to find "the eyes of the blind opened and the ears of the deaf unstopped", and longing to meet those by whose side he had worked and who had so long gone before, you catch an echo of the songs of the celestial country.'[28]

Despite, or because of, the rigours of life at Cowley, Benson's order grew. In its day Cowley was one of the most successful of Anglican male foundations, with overseas houses and a membership including some well-known scholarly writers, an aspect continued until recently by the late Father Christopher Bryant both in his own writings and in his periodical *New Fire*. Cowley remains influential although it has retrenched under the impact of decline in vocations and rising costs. The Cowley property was taken over by the Catholic theological college, St Stephen's House, in the 1980s, and the Fathers withdrew their main base to Westminster.

The Anglican Benedictines had begun with Father Ignatius. Another Benedictine foundation began in 1893, when Benjamin Fearnley Carlyle was clothed as an oblate in the chapel of Nugee's Order of St Augustine. Obsessed with monasticism since his schooldays, he was then a nineteen-year-old medical student, and had already drawn up plans for a threefold Anglican order. But his plans were not put into effect until 1896, when he and some other young men began a community, which was constantly on the move because of local hostility until it settled at Caldey Island off the Pembroke coast in 1906.[29]

Disputes arose in 1911 over the status of the monastery, since it was located on an offshore island. It was visited by Bishop Gore of Oxford who, shocked at the Romish practices he found, demanded an end to the use of the Roman rite, observation of feasts such as the Immaculate Conception and the Assumption of our Lady, and Exposition and Benediction of the Blessed Sacrament. According to some contemporary commentators Gore handled the whole affair tactlessly; but the end result was that the Abbot and twenty-two brothers seceded to Rome in March 1913. They continued to live on the island as a Roman community until 1928, when they moved to Prinknash in Gloucestershire, where a large modern monastery now stands. Caldey is now occupied by Belgian Trappists who among other things make perfume which is sold in a fashionable boutique opposite Brompton Oratory in London.

Three monks remained in the Church of England, and formed the basis for a continuing Benedictine presence within Anglicanism. They moved to Pershore in Worcestershire in 1914, and in 1926, because of growing numbers, to Nashdom in Buckinghamshire, where a mansion built for Russian aristocrats became their new home. The chapel was in the former ballroom. An American priory was set up at Three Rivers, Michigan, in 1939.

A number of male foundations were begun towards the end of the nineteenth century: the Order of St Paul in 1889, the Community of the Resurrection (also known as CR or the Mirfield Fathers) in 1892, the Society of the Sacred Mission in 1894, and the first Franciscan community, the Society of the Divine Compassion, in the same year. All four of these were active orders engaged in evangelistic or missionary work, and partly inspired by the fashionable Christian socialism of the day. The SDC began when a group of Anglican priests dubious of the various schemes for social reform proposed by the Labour party and its associated groups went to live among the poor in the East End of London. They looked after victims of the smallpox epidemics of 1901 and 1902 on hospital ships moored in the Thames and in the special isolation hospital put up on Dagenham Marshes which held four hundred people. The problems encountered are graphically chronicled in works such as Fr Andrew's *Life and Letters*, and the group persisted until the 1950s.

There were a number of other Franciscan foundations: the Society of the Incarnation of the Eternal Son established in 1894, the Community of St Francis (1905), the order of St

Elizabeth of Hungary (1912), and the Brotherhood of St Francis
of Assisi (1921).[30] In 1931, the brotherhood became an officially recognized order within the Church of England when
the Bishop of Salisbury accepted the vows of the first three
brothers. Homes for vagrants were set up in various parts of
the country, the first at Sherborne in 1928, with others in
Cornwall, Wiltshire, Hampshire, Sussex, Hertfordshire and
North and South Wales. An attempt was also made to begin a
brotherhood in India which would express itself in terms of
Indian culture: dress, food, customs. One active figure in this
was Father Algy Robertson, who later returned to England and
began a branch of the Indian brotherhood at St Ives, Hunts.
This was linked with the Dorset community in 1937.

During the Second World War the demand for care of way-
farers decreased, but new work appeared, responsibility for
the Dorset boys' remand home and parishes in Cambridge and
Peckham. When the remand work ended after the war, work
with maladjusted boys took its place, and work in Stepney
replaced that in Peckham. This continued until Cable Street
was demolished in 1961. The Friars then took over the house
of the Society of the Divine Compassion in Plaistow. The
monastery of St Mary at the Cross founded by Father William
Sirr became a centre for training novices. Work in New Guinea
was begun in 1959, a new English house was opened at
Alnmouth, Northumberland, in 1961, and an Australian house
near Brisbane in 1964. Care for vagrants continues, and the
friary has a constantly changing population of boys from
Borstal and alcoholics attempting to reform. In this way the
tradition which began sixty years ago is continued.

Between 1966 and 1969, the Franciscans like other orders
were affected by the spirit of change then current. The
meaning of the religious life was being questioned, loss of
vocation was common, even among those who had spent many
years in the orders, and there were problems of recruitment,
leading to the ageing of the societies – a factor which had
affected the Society of the Divine Compassion. The Franciscans
responded by a revision of their office to a fourfold pattern, and
by liturgical experiment with the new Mass rites at Hilfield. The
distinction between ordained and lay members was de-empha-
sized by the decision to refer to all members of the first order,
priest or lay, as 'brother' or by their Christian name. All offices
were opened to both priests and laymen. A new form of
devolved authority to deal with expansion was worked out,
whereby ministers provincial looked after local work, while

being responsible to a minister general. The expansion continued with new outposts in a number of provincial cities.

The Community of the Resurrection[51] is particularly interesting because it involves a departure from the previous pattern of Anglican male foundations, perhaps due to the commitments of those who created it. Geoffrey Moorhouse calls it a classic example of the specifically Anglican strain which adapts the principles of the religious life to a Church of England setting, as opposed to that which reproduces as far as possible the traditional Catholic ways.[32] CR was founded by Charles Gore when superior of Pusey House, Oxford. Gore was both a liberal Catholic and a socialist very much concerned with contemporary social problems. His community aimed to capture the essence of early Christianity and to present it in a modern form. A liberal approach was apparent in the organizational arrangements of the new community: vows of obedience were to be taken for thirteen months, renewable yearly, not for life, and brethren were only required to have the 'intention' to remain permanently; they were under obedience to their superior but only in a general sense – they could appeal to the higher authority of General Chapter. Nothing was to be required of any brother that violated his conscience, and he was to be free to leave at the end of any year. Material possessions were to be given to the common fund, but not capital. The 'intention' must be to remain celibate, but again this was not a lifelong undertaking. Brothers would not wear monastic dress, but that of the ordinary clergy i.e. cassocks. The terminology employed was novel: 'probationers' rather than 'novices', 'dining-room' rather than 'refectory', 'Senior' rather than 'Superior'. Randall Davidson dubiously remarked that it was the attempt to combine incompatibles – individual liberty and corporate authority. The community response was sharp: that is what the Church of England has been trying to do for the last four hundred years. And CR was to expand both through overseas houses and through the theological college which has since trained many Anglican ordinands.

CR combined ritualism and socialism. The ritualism attracted the usual Protestant hostility, including a visit from Kensit and leaflets denouncing the intention of the Mirfield monks to 'entrap our wives into the hateful confessional'. The socialism was expressed in the continued protests of the brethren against low wages, factory conditions and bad housing, and in the theatre made out of a quarry where Labour leaders such as Keir Hardie spoke, and radical voices such as that of Mrs Pankhurst were also heard.

In recent times Mirfield has survived despite internal difficulties of a kind experienced by many orders in the 1960s and after. It continues to express a distinctive approach to the religious life which, while criticized by some people of a papalist persuasion, still has considerable attraction within the Catholic movement. Well-known members have included Raymond Raynes, Trevor Huddleston, Martin Jarrett-Kerr, Hugh Bishop, Harry Williams, and the present superior, Eric Simmons.[33]

The religious orders today

As the figures quoted in the introduction to this chapter suggest, over the years Anglican religious orders have displayed a fair degree of instability: some have sprung up, flourished for a time and then collapsed. Others have not even flourished, but have remained solitary and forlorn ventures by an enthusiastic few, or even an individual; the best-known case of the last type is Father William of Glasshampton.[34] Although this is clearly not true of all the orders, a number of which became large in size and persisted for long periods of time, still it was not until 1935 that they were thought to have sufficient general importance to justify the setting up of a central administrative body, the Advisory Council on Religious Communities.

The Church of England has come to value their presence and to pay lip-service to them in conventional terms, but arguably they have been in a sense peripheral to its wider life. According to a number of respondents to my enquiries they may even be an embarrassment in some quarters; it is said that they belong to a traditionalist past not the 'reformed' Catholicism of the 1980s. On the other hand, I have also been told that they still provide the 'spiritual powerhouse' which keeps the parishes going.

Geoffrey Moorhouse claims that Anglican orders have shown a distinctive tolerance for individual conscience, linked to a spirit of social rebellion and engagement in social and political problems. It is doubtful, according to Moorhouse, if Father Trevor Huddleston's battles against apartheid in South Africa would have been possible in a more traditional order, apart from Jesuits and Dominicans.[35] Certainly such an approach would be difficult within Roman Catholicism under a Pope of the present complexion.

In the 1960s there were movements for change throughout the Church which greatly affected the religious orders, in ways ranging from the habit worn by nuns and the form of the liturgy to fundamental constitutional issues of power and authority. Mention has been made earlier of how the Anglican Franciscans in particular attempted to respond to such challenges. A particular problem for Anglican orders was the relative recentness of their foundation. Extensive reforms of the kind which took place seemed odd when the movement had only been in existence for a hundred years, and were impeded if there were still people within the order who remembered the founder and who could object to any change on the basis of tradition. Moorhouse suggests that any change can seem like a betrayal of the revered founder.[36] But as he also points out, St Benedict is still seen in such a way within the Roman Church after fourteen centuries.

In the last two decades some houses have come to the end of their life, while others have survived only as a small number of elderly people who are not being replaced by a new generation of novices. Already a number of the large monastic buildings built in the Victorian period have been sold off or put to other uses, as there were no longer the religious to fill them. As already noted, official church statistics suggest that the numerical changes between 1963 and 1984-85 have been striking. A fall of nearly 38 per cent for women in 21 years is very considerable. Although the total female numbers are at present still well over a thousand, if a decline of this magnitude continues, by the end of the century women's orders will have halved in about 30 years. Changes in men's orders seem more complex. Undoubtedly there has been decline, as the reduction of 11 per cent in priest members of male orders suggests, though because of the increase in lay monks the overall total is unchanged. This pattern is interesting and might be investigated further.

A number of reasons for decline can be suggested. The whole conception of the religious life as traditionally understood has been called in question by the reforms of Vatican 2, which have had an impact on Anglican communities as much as on those of the Roman Catholic church. The liberalization of the rule has permitted the growth of problems of authority and relationships which previously were less apparent. The growth of feminism may have affected recruitment of women. Finally, with the rise of the 'alternative society', the availability of other and perhaps more attractive forms of communal life has also presented a threat to the existence of the Anglican orders.

The picture is not entirely black: new communities have

been set up (for example the Community of the Glorious
Ascension, Bede House, and St Gregory's Retreat in Dyfed),
and orders such as the Franciscans have continued to draw
some young recruits. But probably in the next few years there
will be a continuing decline in overall membership, part of the
pattern of change which is now affecting the Catholic movement.

Despite the reforms, the new groups which have developed
since the beginning of the 1960s, and the evidence of an
interest in communal life, there seems to be a curious absence
of discussion of religious orders in general. This contrasts
sharply with the importance attached to them fifty years ago.
Ollard, writing in 1925, claimed that 'the Church in this
country has seen some catastrophic changes in the last thirteen hundred years, and has passed through some volcanic
upheavals, but in all its exciting story I doubt whether there is
anything more wonderful, more startling in its unexpected-
ness, than the revival of the Religious Orders in the last
century'.[37] Comparable modern statements are not to be
found. Religious orders receive only limited mention in the
literature published at the time of the sesquicentenary of the
Oxford Movement in 1983.[38] This may well reflect a general
uncertainty about their function today.

7

Walsingham

In the wracks of Walsingham
Whom should I chuse?
But the Queene of Walsingham
To be my guide and muse?
Philip, Earl of Arundel

Introduction

Within a sacramental world, some places are especially holy. Religions regularly define numinous landscapes,[1] sacred territories within which the divine power is particularly available. Churches are one example of this; shrines are another. This chapter is about the recovery within Anglicanism of a numinous landscape lost for centuries: England's Nazareth, the holy land of Walsingham.

In attempting a revolution by tradition, the Tractarians and their successors had at their disposal all the conventional apparatus of Catholicism, an important component of which was the cult of Mary. However, this would clearly be one of the more provocative elements in the revival because of its association in popular culture with Roman Catholicism, and therefore with the folk devils of 'Romanizing' and 'popery'. In fact a moderate Marian component had existed in the high church tradition and was continued by the Tractarians. It is expressed in hymns such as Bishop Ken's 'Her Virgin eyes saw God incarnate born' and Keble's 'Ave Maria! blessed Maid!'. But that it was contentious is apparent from the fact that both Pusey and Keble at first rejected any notion of direct prayer to the Blessed Virgin, and from Keble's decision, on the advice of Coleridge and Dyson, to leave out of his *Lyra Innocentium* the verse:

> Therefore, as kneeling day by day
> We to our Father duteous pray
> So unforbidden may we speak

An Ave to Christ's Mother meek,
(As children with 'good morrow' come
To elders in some happy home).

In the ritualistic period, Catholics were far less cautious. Statues of Mary were set up in some of their churches, surrounded by flowers and candles, and Marian prayers were increasingly used. In 1880 the devotional Confraternity of the Children of Mary, later renamed the Confraternity of Our Lady Help of Christians, was founded. In 1903 this became the Confraternity of Our Lady. The Union of the Holy Rosary which had been founded in 1886 was amalgamated with the Confraternity in 1920. In 1904 the League of Our Lady was formed. This combined with the Confraternity in 1931 as the Society of Mary, which is now the main Marian society within the Church of England.

By the early part of the twentieth century, therefore, devotion to Mary was a part of Catholic practice in the Church of England (though far from universal). Marian hymns appeared in the *English Hymnal* of 1906, and prayers such as the Hail Mary, the Angelus and the Regina Coeli were employed, together with the Rosary.[2] But one element lacking was pilgrimage to Marian shrines, a common feature on the continent eagerly observed by peripatetic Anglican Catholics looking for fresh exotica to bring home. In the medieval period, a frequent referent for some sections of the Catholic movement, England had been the home of many shrines, especially those dedicated to the Blessed Virgin. Indeed, as Catholics were soon to emphasize in their propaganda, in the Middle Ages devotion to Mary was so strong, there were so many churches dedicated to her and so many centres of Marian pilgrimage, that England was known as 'Our Lady's Dowry'. It was inevitable that at some stage an attempt would be made to restore devotions of this kind; whether it was successful depended on the setting within which it was attempted and the point in time at which the attempt was made.

Of all the medieval Marian shrines, the largest and best known was Walsingham, which by the twentieth century was merely a small and peaceful village in a remote part of Norfolk, with little trace of its former glories. The revival of the cult of Our Lady of Walsingham from the 1920s onwards illustrates many of the most interesting features of the Catholic movement, especially with regard to the re-enchantment theme. To explain this at the most general level we may employ a cultural argument along lines put forward by Robert Bocock in his pioneering work of the early 1970s on the rituals of industrial society. He suggests that 'the general socio-cultural setting' provides a greater degree of support in the present than was the case in the nineteenth century. Within certain sub-groups in England, of which Anglican Catholicism is one, a 'feminization' of culture has occurred. Virtues regarded as essentially 'female' are given a higher value than in the past. The place of Mary as a central feminine symbol in Christianity, and her veneration, are therefore more acceptable.[3] Further, a specific factor of significance at Walsingham was the personal charisma to which reference has already been made.

The coming of Father Patten

According to legend, in the year 1061 the Virgin Mary appeared to the lady of the manor of Walsingham, Richeldis de Faverches, and took her in spirit to Nazareth. Here she was shown a vision of the house in which the Holy Family had lived, and was commanded to build a replica of this in Walsingham, near a spring which was to become the source of the Holy Well, the waters of which were used for healing. This was the beginning of the shrine of Our Lady of Walsingham to which pilgrims came from all over Europe. It is said to have been more popular than any other shrine of the time and drew the rich and powerful as well as ordinary people. The monarchs of England came on many occasions: Richard Coeur de Lion after his return from imprisonment in the Holy Land, Henry VII after the battle of Stoke, Katharine of Aragon after the victory of Flodden Field. Henry VIII is known to have made at least three pilgrimages, allegedly walking barefoot from the nearby hamlet of Barsham; he paid the wages of a mass priest at Walsingham and had a candle burning in the shrine up to Lady Day, 1538. But then Walsingham suffered the same fate as many other shrines and religious houses in England – it was sacked, its treasures confiscated, and the revered image of Our Lady of Walsingham was taken to London and burnt at Chelsea. The cult was ended for a period of centuries, although there are legends that from time to time mysterious visitors came to Walsingham to pray amid the ruins.

The first mention of Walsingham in the Catholic revival was in the church of St Mary at Buxted in Sussex, one of many built by the prolific Father Wagner. Within the church was a lady chapel, screened off and made to the dimensions of the ancient Holy House at Walsingham. Father Wagner had a great devotion to Mary and dedicated a church to her in Brighton (the Annunciation), but apart from the Buxted chapel appears to have taken no other interest in Walsingham.

The second mention, and one which affected Walsingham itself, was when Charlotte Boyd, a wealthy Catholic interested in the revival of Benedictine monasticism in the Church of England, commenced a plan to buy back for the Church of England all the old monastic property lost at the Reformation. One of the buildings she bought was the Slipper Chapel at Walsingham, a relic of the medieval cult which was then being put to bizarre use as a cowshed. Miss Boyd later became a Roman Catholic, and the Slipper Chapel was to be the focus of the revived Roman devotion to Our Lady of Walsingham, although because of internal disputes it was not used for public services until 1934.

The Anglican parish church at Walsingham had experienced a moderate form of Catholicism from the 1880s onwards. The Lee-Warner family, who were enthusiastic Puseyites, had restored the church according to Tractarian principles, employing the well-known architect Street for this purpose, and in 1882 appointed as vicar the Revd G. R. Woodward, who had been a curate at St Barnabas', Pimlico, the scene of ritual-istic riots. He introduced six candles on the altar, eucharistic vestments, plainsong and also daily sung Evensong. The pattern of worship became an eight o'clock Holy Communion every Sunday, Mattins or Sung Eucharist on alternate Sundays, and Holy Communion on two weekdays and all Prayer Book saints' days. This pattern continued during the following two incumbencies. The first sign of a distinctive Marian interest was when the Revd E. L. Reeves, vicar from 1904 to 1921, installed a small figure of the Blessed Virgin, provided by the League of Our Lady. A greater expression of devotion began with the appointment as vicar of the Revd A. H. Patten in 1921.

Father Patten's role in the revival was of central impor-tance. What he did was set very much within the established framework of the Catholic movement: Marian devotion had been revived and there were existing cultic groups to provide a nucleus of pilgrims. Thus there was in a sense an unsatisfied need, a missing element in the Catholic economy which he set about meeting: a centre for the Marian cult. But arguably it needed a personality like Patten to get it going and to persist despite initial difficulties and continuing problems. Thus he is a focal figure in the story of Walsingham and deserves further consideration.

To begin with, his childhood and youth was deeply influenced by the Catholic revival. He fully accepted the values and beliefs of Catholicism and was committed to their advance. Secondly, he was part of a network of Catholic enthusiasts whose acquaintance he had made during his early years, so that at crucial points in the development of the Walsingham cult he was able to draw upon the resources which they could provide. Thirdly, he was an intensely charismatic personality, a natural actor, likeable and possessed of a personal authority which enabled him to achieve what might not have been possible for a more retiring man.

His initial task was to gain his parishioners' support. In part this was eased by the traditional loyalty to the church found especially at that time in many rural areas. But Father Patten did much for himself, building up personal attachments by his frequent visiting and power of attraction. A small number of supporters lived with him at the vicarage and set the tone for the changes which he wished to introduce, and his servers and their girl friends were always welcome to his house, where they would have supper and games on a Sunday evening. Thus he built up a nucleus of support in the village, and established a reputation as a 'character', either cycling around the village with his cassock tucked up around his waist, or being driven about in a little pony trap.

His single-mindedness and ability to transmit his vision appears to have been his most important characteristic. Throughout his life he was capable of painting word pictures which grasped the imagination and enthused others – at least until they compared Patten's vision with the world they knew. 'I well remember how one Saturday evening, along the sunken road returning from St Mary's, I discussed with Father the meaning of the Catholic Church. As he explained it, it was lucid and wonderful, but when related to the existing situation outside Walsingham, and in particular in the protestant-dominated parishes where I laboured, it bore no relation to reality.'[1] But as Colin Stephenson rightly remarks, '. . . if he had not had this single eye which would only see things as he wished them to be, he would not have been able to create what he did.'[5]

Church life in the village was transformed first. The 'Interim Rite', which rearranged the Prayer Book liturgy in a Roman form, was introduced, and much of it was said silently. The

Blessed Sacrament was reserved despite opposition from the bishop. Incense was introduced into services. Statues of the Sacred Heart and St Anthony of Padua were installed in the church. The model much of the time was continental Roman Catholicism as Patten had observed it in France and Belgium. 'The amazing thing is that he managed to get the villagers to follow suit and behave like continentals in their religion. They came to Confession in surprising numbers, and before Festivals and on Saturday evenings the church would be full of those waiting to be shriven; 7.30 a.m. on Sunday mornings was reserved for men's confessions, and they came. He made great demands and these villagers, in a part of England always regarded as traditionally puritan, rose to them . . . when he started reservation he expected them to keep a watch before the Tabernacle all day, – a practice that continued for several years. He encouraged them to come to the weekday services and got a response which never failed to astonish those who came to Walsingham for the first time. Devotions, such as Stations of the Cross in Lent, became a tradition of the village and continued to be observed, so that even after his death people who had more or less lapsed from coming to Mass would still appear at Stations. There is no doubt that, whatever he accomplished later, the work of those first few years as parish priest of Walsingham was the most outstanding and compares with the greatest evangelistic work recorded of the heroes of the Catholic revival.'[6]

The revival of the cult

Father Patten had come to Walsingham feeling that it was his duty to revive the cult of our Lady. He began by having a more appropriate image carved to provide a focus of devotion, and on 6 July 1922 this was installed on a pillar in the guilds chapel of the parish church during a conference for local priests. Setting the style for later extravaganzas, the image was carried in procession by village girls dressed in white, escorted by other girls carrying branches of syringa while the church bells were pealed. The statue was blessed and a sermon was preached. From that day on the Rosary was recited every evening before the image and a book of intercessions was started; these were read out at that time, and the whole devotion acquired the title of 'Shrine Prayers'.

The first pilgrimage was nearly a disaster: the numbers coming were greatly over-estimated, and there arrived on the

London train only 'a very large priest and two very small
ladies'.[7] But, undeterred, Father Patten arranged for all the
villagers who could come to take part, and thus the first
pilgrimage was made by the villagers themselves. Later
pilgrimages under the sponsorship of the League of our Lady
were better supported and became a regular event twice a
year in May and August.

By 1925, numbers attending events at the shrine were growing. In August 100 pilgrims came from outside Walsingham to
attend the 'Ecumenical August Feast'. Father Patten wrote
somewhat defensively that 'all ages and all classes were represented, while the presence of a retired Judge and a goodly
muster of the more robust sex made any outside comment of
exotic devotions suitable for ladies and sacristy-minded youths,
utterly untrue'.[8]

In 1925 the Society of our Lady of Walsingham was founded:
members wore a blue scapular and their names were recorded
in a book kept at the feet of the image. The intention of the
Society was to unify members and to provide further support
for the shrine. In January 1926 a quarterly paper for members
of the Society was started. A Walsingham Clergy Fund was set
up in London under the inspiration of Father Fynes-Clinton of
St Magnus the Martyr, London Bridge, to provide an assistant
priest and supplement the small stipend of the living. Further
financial help was provided by the sisters. In 1927 the priest
associates group was formed; members were to say Mass on
Saturday with intention for Walsingham.

The growth of the cult was dependent on certain key
figures. Fynes-Clinton was one of these; another was Sir
William Milner, an architect from a wealthy family in Yorkshire, whom Father Patten had first met through the League of
our Lady in 1922. Patten was not a good financial manager and
frequently ran into debt. Sir William helped him out regularly,
and also provided funds for various developments, including
the 'Hospice of our Lady Star of the Sea', which was created
out of a large house, some cottages and outbuildings
purchased for £1,750 in 1926.

Walsingham began to acquire some notoriety. On 1 September 1926 the Bishop of Durham, Hensley Henson, (noted
earlier for his attack on ritualizers at an ordination in 1920),
published an article on pilgrimage in the *Evening Standard* in
which he criticized the Walsingham revival. He had visited
Walsingham on 17 August, i.e. at Assumptiontide, when he
would have found it at its most colourful. According to

Henson, Walsingham was 'as complete an example of triumphant Anglo-Catholicism as the country can present'. But 'it would probably be an error to attach much importance to the revived pilgrimages, which are rather "pageants" than religious acts. The pitiable rubbish of the Walsingham processional hymn could only be intelligible as part of a "pageant". As an act of religion it would be profane.' This article was reprinted in *Our Lady's Mirror* with some caustic comment. Colin Stephenson records that Henson's published letters show that he revisited Walsingham several times. He appears to have been fascinated by what he refers to in Trollopian terms as 'this revolting illegality'.

Objections also came predictably from Protestants, both through protest in the village and through Parliament, where a peer heckled the Bishop of Norwich, Bertram Pollock, while he was speaking in the Lords on obedience to the Prayer Book. It was as a consequence of the cry of 'What about Walsingham?' that Pollock made a personal visitation to the parish church, where the Catholic innovations shocked him greatly, and he ordered that they should all be removed. Patten refused, but mentioned the possibility that the image of our Lady might be transferred to a separate chapel built on private property. He had been thinking of this for some time because of his concern that, as was often the case with Catholic innovations, all that he had achieved might be reversed by a later incumbent. After an appeal for funds to build such a chapel, by spring 1931 £700 had been raised, and Sir William Milner contributed the balance to finance a reproduction of the original medieval Holy House within which the image had rested, which would be covered by a larger chapel.

On the site which was chosen for the building were found both a cobbled courtyard like that mentioned by Erasmus in his account of the medieval shrine dated 1511, and a Saxon well which had been filled in, and which when excavated was found to contain refuse of the Tudor period. Father Patten was convinced that this showed the site chosen to be that of the original shrine; others were not.

After the building of the new Holy House the shrine grew further. A college of guardians with its own constitution was set up. Many leading figures of the Catholic movement became Guardians: Sir William Milner; Bishop O'Rorke; Father Fynes-Clinton; the Abbot of Nashdom; the Revd A. H. Baverstock, vicar of Hinton Martel in Dorset, a rural Catholic outpost; the Revd Elton Lury, vicar of St Peter's Limehouse, (who was married but admitted as a guardian although the constitution did not permit this; it was ignored); the Revd Humphrey Whitby of St Mary's, Graham Street; the Revd Roger Wodehouse of St Paul's, Oxford; the Duke of Argyll; Lord Halifax; Sir John Best-Shaw; and the Revd Derrick Lingwood, a village boy who had been trained for the priesthood at Father Patten's prompting and who was to become pilgrimage secretary and financial manager of the shrine.

On Thursday, 15 October 1931, at seven o'clock the new chapel was aspersed and blessed, and the deeds were handed over to the trustees. At 11.30 there was a High Mass in the parish church. In the afternoon there was Benediction, followed by the procession of the statue from the parish church to the new building in the presence of about 3,000 people. The procession was over half a mile long. By now there were 134 priest associates and many of these attended. Both the Abbot of Nashdom and Bishop O'Rorke were present, plus a number of monks, nuns and friars.

In subsequent weeks visitors came from all over the country, and the grounds of the new shrine began to be turned into the beautiful gardens which they are today, a combination of the ideas of Father Patten and the work of William Frary, a villager who besides being gardener was also beadle of the shrine. In the gardens were erected Stations of the Cross and a Calvary, a large crucifix and a carrilon of bells. The Holy House contained the image, above the altar in a niche surrounded by rays of glory on a wall hung with cloth of gold. In the walls were set stones from ruined abbeys and holy places all over the British Isles, and just outside the House the newly discovered Holy Well was located.

By the autumn of 1932, plans for further extensions were under way. The initial suggestion was that there should be a choir, to be built in time for the centenary of the Oxford Movement in 1933, but sufficient support for this was not forthcoming. In 1936, however, a gift of about £4,500 enabled the start of the pilgrimage church as it stands today, with grandiose ideas worked out in a relatively small space. Father Patten wanted fifteen altars, one for every mystery of the Rosary. There were insufficient funds to build this on an adequate scale, and the final result was small and cramped: 146 feet long by 60 feet wide at the widest part. Little chapels for which various Anglican devotional societies are responsible are tucked in behind every pillar, and priests have complained that the altars are so small that it is actually physically uncomfortable to say Mass at them. There is a dim religious light (reduced somewhat by extensions since 1970), out of which loom numerous statues; the walls are a riot of colour, with murals by various artists, most notably Enid Chadwick.

Critics have seen this church as an absurdity. Certainly it is hard to justify on the grounds of extra accommodation suggested by Father Patten, for it provides only limited additional space. But to concentrate on the functional aspects is to miss the point. The shrine church, consecrated in 1938, is above all else an achievement of the imagination, an icon of the Catholic vision. To visit it with a sympathetic openness to atmosphere is to experience this vision, whether one accepts it or not.

The development of pilgrimage

By the outbreak of war in 1939, the cult of our Lady of Walsingham was firmly established. There were now 200 priest associates, and the Whit Monday pilgrimage had drawn 6,000 visitors. In the whole of 1938 it was estimated that there had been 80,000 visitors, including Roman Catholics. But, impressive though the changes had been – it had taken only seventeen years to move from the statue in the guilds chapel in 1921 to the fully-fledged pilgrim church of 1938, from a handful of visitors to crowds numbered in thousands – the shrine still had a relatively small constituency: a part of the Catholic movement which was itself only a part of the Church of England.

The stability of the shrine was threatened by this and by a number of other factors. It was still the subject of Protestant harassment from time to time. It was rejected by the Roman Catholics, who had set up a rival shrine at the Slipper Chapel in 1934, and who with their larger resources were able to stage pilgrimages of far greater size than Father Patten. The income of the Anglican shrine was small, so financial crises were constant; Father Patten had written in 1932, 'We long for the day when England's Nazareth is solvent'. Finally it was a one man band, Father Patten's creation and sustained by his imagination and energy. What would happen when he went? The first steps towards dealing with this had been taken with the creation of the College of Guardians.

During the war, although the flow of pilgrims was reduced to a trickle, there were fresh developments: a children's home from St Hilary in Cornwall was transferred to Walsingham to escape Protestant aggression, and became another element in the strengthening of the shrine. In 1944 a choir school was set up, and continued in a somewhat unstable fashion until 1956; there were conflicts over successive headmasters' purely educational aims and Father Patten's view of it as an adjunct of the shrine. Father Patten also encouraged the development of local Walsingham groups for people who could not make the journey in wartime, and the 'spiritual pilgrimage to Walsingham' was devised. By spring 1950 there were twenty such groups with a membership ranging from 11 to 60.

With the end of the war, small pilgrimages were resumed. In 1950 1,000 lay visitors were recorded for the Whit Monday pilgrimage, plus 50 priests. Other developments making for greater security in the future took place. There was an attempt to establish a community to work with Father Patten at the shrine, and between 1945 and 1955 sixteen men tried their vocation to this life. But it was not successful: personal and interpersonal problems were too great, and the venture finally collapsed.

In 1949, Sir William Milner made over his estate in Yorkshire to the shrine, providing a new source of income. This paid for the conversion of some derelict cottages as a home for retired priests, which again showed Father Patten's creative genius, as a range of buildings were established round a quadrangle with a garden in the middle, with bed-sitting rooms and a refectory of very medieval appearance. But few priests came, and there were no special provisions for looking after them. In 1954 the Sisters of St Margaret began to build a permanent convent in the shrine grounds. This is of a very different style to the shrine buildings; the Reverend Mother approvingly compared it to a council house. Disenchantment was emerging (symbolically at any rate) even at Walsingham.

But in the early fifties the major event, the Whit Monday national pilgrimage drew between one and two thousand pilgrims, with small parish pilgrimages becoming more common throughout a season which ran from April to September. Patten was concerned with the continuation of the shrine, and published an article entitled, 'What will happen when Father Patten dies?' This foresaw the appointment of a new administrator while pointing out that 'it will never be quite the same, of course, because a new man could not possibly maintain a tradition which he had not helped to create, and after his term of office had expired, a new man, a new tradition, will replace the old'.[9] This is a very interesting article, showing that Father Patten was highly conscious, despite all that had been achieved so far, of the instability of his enterprise. He saw the answer in the revitalizing of his Community of St Augustine, but despite his appeals this did not prove possible. Moreover, rules of his own devising worked against him, as when the bursar, Father Lingwood, his principal assistant, who had been trained by Patten for ordination in his youth, left, partly because he was out of sympathy with some aspects of the shrine policy, and later married. Since priest guardians were required to be celibate, Father Lingwood was de facto excluded by his marriage, and the rule was not waived as it had been in the case of Father Lury in 1931. The issue was discussed by the guardians. Some felt that the rule ought to be disregarded in Father Lingwood's case because of his special position in the revival, and an amendment was put forward to alter the constitution of the College of Guardians. Father Patten appears to have taken the proposal as an attack upon his work in general and opposed it strongly. After some internal politicking, it was decided that the requirement to resign on marriage should be dropped, but that the constitution should otherwise remain unchanged. This dispute is another indication that the new spirit of postwar Catholicism was manifesting itself even in such an apparently reactionary place as Walsingham. Some of the newer guardians were less attached to every element of tradition than their predecessors, and were concerned that Walsingham should become a more open institution, for the whole Church rather than for a small minority of enthusiasts within it.

Numbers continued to grow, and an appeal was launched to set up a proper endowment for priests' stipends. A cell of the Society of our Lady of Walsingham was set up in the House of Commons and the Speaker's Chaplain said Mass for members in St Stephen's chapel in the House. Further new building was carried out: the hospice was extended and a large gatehouse was built, also a new chapel for the convent. In 1956, the jubilee year of the rebuilding of the Holy House was celebrated with a gathering in Caxton Hall in London attended by about 400 people, and a fiesta at Walsingham, including a torchlight procession to the parish church, High Mass at midnight and Exposition of the Sacrament throughout the night, with Mass said at half-hourly intervals in the Holy House, and a procession through the village the following day.

In 1958, the bishops were to meet for the Lambeth Conference, and the first bishops' pilgrimage was arranged. On 11 August this began, but at the conclusion of Benediction that evening, Father Patten collapsed and died at the age of 73. He was buried with elaborate ceremonial, and a private valedictory from one person who had known the shrine well: 'Considering his many limitations, it is amazing that A.H.P. managed to create the whole Walsingham racket and that it should have survived his decease'.[10] But the argument of this chapter is that neither the creation of the shrine nor its persistence are quite so surprising as might at first appear. On the contrary, without belittling Father Patten's accomplishments in any way, I have suggested that the social conditions for the establishment of such an institution were right in the 1920s, and it is probable that it could not have been established later.[11] Once established it found an expanding constituency. The momentum of its support has sustained it, and permitted both growth and change, in a climate which has been very hard for the Church in many other areas.

Walsingham since the 1960s

A new period now began in the short history of the shrine. Father Patten's successor was Colin Stephenson, formerly a naval chaplain and Vicar of the 'advanced' church of St Mary Magdalen, Oxford. He rationalized the operations of the shrine to some extent. It is from the beginning of his period as administrator that records of organized annual attendances are available. In the ten years following Father Patten's death numbers were fairly steady: between 5,000 and 6,000 a year. The national pilgrimage, which had averaged 1,500 to 2,000 in the 1950s rose to over 5,000 in 1959, and settled down to an average of 2,500–3,000 in the 1960s. By 1968 there were about 80 priest associates, 1,000 members of the Society of Our Lady of Walsingham, and 3,000 Friends of Walsingham (an attachment which did not involve commitment to a rule of life). The quarterly *Walsingham Review* (successor to *Our Lady's Mirror*) had a circulation of 4,500. Roughly 75 per cent of pilgrims were female. Altogether, in the late 1960s, about 100,000 Anglicans came annually, while large numbers of Roman Catholics visited the steadily growing Roman shrine at the Slipper Chapel. There were also numerous coach tours to what was regarded as one of the 'sights' of the area.

Colin Stephenson sought to 'bring the shrine into the Church of England' by establishing better relationships both with the diocese of Norwich and more widely throughout the Church. Walsingham had been regarded as a curiosity, a thing apart, a different religion from 'ordinary C. of E.', and he tried to alter this view by making personal contact with nearby churches where he officiated at services according to local custom, by arranging for the rural deanery to meet at the shrine, and by improving relations with the bishop. It was as a result of this that the shrine acquired responsibility for several rural parishes in the area. Improved relations were immediately apparent at the 1959 national pilgrimage, which was also part of the Church Union centenary celebrations, when the High Mass was celebrated in the abbey grounds with greatly. increased numbers, and attended by the Bishop of Thetford as representative of the diocesan bishop. At a later stage, Father Stephenson was made an honorary canon of Norwich and elected by the diocesan clergy to represent them as a Proctor in Convocation. All these changes expanded the shrine's support. Now referred to as 'the shrine of the Incarnation', it could appeal to a much broader constituency.

During his ten-year period as administrator Colin Stephenson travelled extensively throughout Britain and abroad publicizing Walsingham, as did the assistant clergy whom the shrine was now able to engage. The numbers of pilgrims grew considerably, and the pilgrimage season which had previously ended in September now extended further into the autumn. More extensions to the buildings were necessary: the hospice was remodelled with more comfortable accommodation, and a new refectory and kitchens were built. All this was in a contemporary style; so quite soon after Father Patten's death the modernizing pattern, begun with the new convent in 1954, was extended. A chantry chapel of All Souls was built in 1965, also to a modern design.

The liturgical and other changes in the early 1960s provoked conflicts between traditionalists and innovators within the Catholic movement. Walsingham was caught up in this because of its image as a sanctuary for reaction in some quarters, and because of the willingness of Father Stephenson and others to experiment with new ideas: he began a Mass facing the people in 1965. The Walsingham sisters also took up some of the new ideas.

The previous hostility between the two shrines, Anglican and Roman Catholic, began to abate, and in 1965 attendance at the others' pilgrimages began. In 1967 a conference on the place of Mary in Christian theology was attended by Anglicans, Catholics, Orthodox and Free Churchmen, and an Ecumenical Society of the Blessed Virgin Mary was formed.

All these changes can be regarded as positive, but others

might be seen as less so. There was a decline in the fervour
which the shrine generated in its adherents. A number of those
who had known it for a long time commented that by the late
1960s there was what one person called 'a definite loss of
atmosphere': in the changed environment he often found it
difficult to say his prayers. Perhaps as a reflection of the unease
caused by change, several respondents told me that they
thought the priests were less friendly and approachable, while
priests commented on the monotony of the pilgrimage season
and the demands made on them. Both sets of responses may
well have been the outcome of the transition which the shrine
was undergoing.

As the seventies advanced there was a continuing growth in
numbers and increasing ecumenical activity. In 1976, there
were approximately 200 separate pilgrimage groups, between
January and November. On 11 May 1980, Cardinal Hume led a
party of 10,000. A fortnight later Archbishop Runcie preached
to 15,000 at the national pilgrimage.[12] From 1981 onwards the
pilgrimage season had begun with a joint Eucharist celebrated
by the staffs of the two shrines. At the Carmelite convent in
Quidenham, three Anglican and three Roman priests con-
celebrated at the same altar, then moved to separate altars for
the words of consecration (which were synchronized) and the
Communion.[13] This was part of an interdenominational retreat
which also involved the divine office of the community and
exposition of the sacrament. A second retreat was held at All
Hallows', Ditchingham in 1982. The Carmel of our Lady of
Walsingham was founded in 1982. There nuns live a life which
according to one popular account is 'silent and solitary, frugal
and disciplined'.[14] A joint pilgrimage of 650 pilgrims was led by
the Anglican Bishop of Chester and the Roman Catholic Bishop
of Arundel and Brighton to celebrate the thirteenth centenary
of St Wilfred's evangelization of Sussex.[15] In May 1982, the two
administrators took the statue of our Lady of Walsingham to
Wembley where it was placed on the altar in front of 80,000
pilgrims while the Pope celebrated mass. An ecumenical
service attended by approximately 1,000 people in which both
administrators took part was televised from the Chapel of
Reconciliation attached to the Slipper Chapel on 15 August
1982. This had been consecrated by the Roman Bishop Clark of
East Anglia on 22 May before a congregation of all denominations.[16]

Two very recent events which demonstrate the changed
status of the shrine occurred in October 1985. On the fourth

day of that month the Duchess of Kent opened St Joseph's, a hospice wing for sick and handicapped pilgrims. On the 18th October, Fr David Hope, Master of the College of Guardians was consecrated bishop of Wakefield. Walsingham has come a long way since the first pilgrimage made by one very large priest and two very small ladies in 1923. Sixty years later it has been estimated that in all half a million people visit the two shrines every year.[17] While an unknown proportion of these are casual visitors, curious but with no religious motive, a substantial number are not. The Walsingham shrine is an extraordinary and under-rated twentieth century expression of the Catholic vision, and continues to develop under the present administrator, Father Christopher Colven.

The significance of Walsingham

Robert Bocock interprets the growth of Walsingham and other Marian shrines in Britain as one expression of an increasingly 'feminized' culture, along with the enhanced position of women and the development of anti-war sentiments. He also cites the steady shift within Anglicanism towards the Catholic end of the religious spectrum since the end of the nineteenth century.[18]

Another approach is suggested by the writings of David Martin. He notes how 'England . . . is full of sacred plots and holy corners alive with Arthurian promises and dreams. Avalon in England and Avallon in France are mysterious numinous landscapes, only half hiding their secret life. . . . Every land builds its sacred city and sanctifies a holy of holies, specially dear and unique to itself . . . it can be a holy island, holy mountain, holy stone, embalmed body or sacred image.'[19] Such shrines are closely tied in with conceptions of national identity. When the image of the Virgin in Andorra was destroyed by fire in 1973, it 'was accounted a national disaster. The Virgin stood for God and country: she was the sacred guardian of place, the protector of the city. Both radical signs, the Virgin and the city, colluded as agents of identity, of locality and conservation.'[20]

This perspective can be applied to Walsingham, which recapitulates a series of potent images in English religious culture and engages with that culture through a number of symbols of national identity. In this sense the Walsingham cult is analogous to that of the Virgin of Andorra.

To begin with there is the journey. For the pilgrim this is not an ordinary journey, even if undertaken by conventional means.

Pilgrims travel to Walsingham, especially for the first time, with varying degress of curiosity, apprehension, enthusiasm or indifference, but at the very least they are aware that they are on a pilgrimage, and this may be brought home to them, especially if they travel in an organized party, by the observances undertaken on the way. Some groups walk there over a number of days, sometimes carrying a cross. Others travel by coach or train, and again may take more than one day to get there. The journey is given a religious framework: hymns are sung, prayers are said, most notably the Rosary, and services are held at stops. The party often halts overnight in a church hall, or a convent; the setting then is religious. Mass is said at the beginning of each day. The daily offices of Matins or Evensong may be recited, and the day may conclude with Compline or Benediction. According to David Martin the medieval travelling pilgrim is 'thrust into liminality'; he enters a realm of other-worldliness. 'He is both native and alien, moving between one condition and another, shifting through gradations of sanctity.'[21] This is made apparent as the visitor approaches the shrine often referred to as 'England's Nazareth'. A number of visual symbols demarcate the passage into the sacred territory. The landscape acquires a new and distinctive shape. In the last few miles there is a physical transition from the bustle of the railway or the motorway to the quiet of country lanes and rural landscape. At East Barsham the Tudor manor house stands sentinel-like at the roadside; on the outskirts of Walsingham the sweeping roof of the Roman Catholic Chapel of Reconciliation, built like a Norfolk barn, is visible across the fields, and soon after the ruins of the medieval Franciscan friary. The pilgrim is often urged to maintain silence and to offer a mental intention for the visit. Individuals may walk the last mile or so. A definite boundary is symbolized in such ways, and the crossing of it implies entry into a different state of being, into the holy land of Walsingham.

One writer suggests that many pilgrims see Walsingham as a sort of Brigadoon, which disappears as soon as they leave.[22] Walsingham is still, despite the scatter of shops selling religious bric-a-brac along the main street, recognizably a traditional Norfolk village, with quaint little brick cottages, a village pump-cum-lock-up, a Shire Hall, a ruined abbey, and gardens full of flowers and well-tended lawns. It is surrounded by parkland, with grass of a rich green and majestic trees, and outside major pilgrimages it is relatively free of traffic. The railway station was closed before Beeching and has been

turned into an Orthodox monastery, there are few cars and
even fewer buses. At night there is a penetrating silence,
through which, in winter, you can hear the ice cracking in the
trees. At Christmas houses have illuminated cribs in the
window, and it is easy to imagine that Christ could have been
born in a place such as this, perhaps in one of the stables
which must lie somewhere in the town. The stars seem huge
and close. In spring or summer, when most people go, the
wind blows gently through the trees by the parish church and
along the sunken lane, the grass is lush and the gardens of the
shrine are bright with flowers. The shrine church and its
surrounding buildings have a striking, if misleading, patina of
age. The pilgrim *is* in a 'holy land'. A range of powerful images
of the rural, and history, and through these of national identity,
are evoked.

Walsingham, like a Roman counterpart such as Aylesford in
Kent, is unmistakably an *English* shrine. It summons up the
range of communal values associated with the pre-industrial
ages of faith, and embodies a potent myth. *In illo tempore*,
before the industrial age had destroyed community, we all lived
in places such as Walsingham, focused around the church,
where national unity and religious unity, communal loyalty and
loyalty to our maker were fused in one great symbol of belonging, the holy Eucharist. For the pilgrim the landscape of
Walsingham has been sacralized.

Simultaneously Walsingham generates both an individual
religiosity, and a sense of solidarity with fellow Catholics. The
individualism is inherent in the personal nature of the experience of pilgrimage. The pilgrim makes his confession; goes to
Mass and receives Communion; bows his head before the sacrament at Benediction; prays by himself in a quiet chapel 'where
prayer has been valid';[23] is sprinkled with holy water from the
well and perhaps takes a bottle back home (over 50,000 are
supplied every summer), to be kept on the bedside table or in
the medicine cabinet; venerates a relic by kissing the reliquary
which the priest holds out to him. In all these activities the
pilgrim is alone before God, who seems specially present in
this sacred place. The dim religious atmosphere created by
Father Patten lends itself perfectly to the creation of a sense of
the divine presence in the church, and also, archetypally for
England, in the gardens.

The results of this experience will vary. For a few it is a first
step on the way to priesthood or convent. Others join one of
the Walsingham groups and attend meetings in their home

area. For others it is the source of ultimate meaning: 'Walsingham showed me that all my doubts about God were silly; I experienced his presence.'[24] There are the cures, less recorded now, of deafness, lupus, lameness, arthritis, skin trouble, a knee injury, nerves, tuberculosis. The point of these for this study is not their medical status but the meaning which was given to them: the help of our Lady of Walsingham.

Walsingham also has a collective aspect, the generation of sociability and solidarity. Many of the activities take place in groups: worship, talking, eating, drinking. There is a great deal of laughter, both within the sacred context of worship and outside it. People experience a sense of belonging, of having roots. 'As a lay member of the Society I feel very much a "part" of the Shrine', one respondent wrote. Another spoke of the 'enormous atmosphere of friendliness' to be found among all the pilgrims and clergy. The charismatic element appears in recollections of Father Stephenson 'holding court' in the shrine grounds, with a cup of tea in one hand, gesturing grandly with the other, or Father Fynes-Clinton 'keeping a group of girls spellbound'.

For the Catholic movement as a whole, Walsingham is of great importance. It has to be extreme. As a priest said some years ago, 'We want it to scream at people because it's saying something extraordinary, that God took flesh.'[25] The interpersonal tensions behind the scenes to which Colin Stephenson refers in his books may be recognized or not; if they are, they are not central. In the minds of Catholics, Walsingham stands for the reality of the Incarnation, and of the immanent presence of Christ today. Latterly it also symbolizes the growing unity between Christians, as the former hostility between denominations declines, and Anglicans, Roman Catholics, Orthodox and Free Church come together to share in worship and social activity. The increasing attraction of the shrine to large numbers of people makes it easy to understand why it can be claimed that 'at Walsingham the ages of faith are now'.[26]

8

Catholic Socialism

Baptism was the entrance of every human being into the greatest democratic society in the world. The Mass was the weekly meeting of a society of rebels against a Mammon-worshipping order. Let the working men of England claim their rights as Christ's soldiers and the present world-order would crumble. . . . It was because England had ceased to be Christian that injustice and sweating and cruelty stalked the country. Let the true church, the baptised democracy, enter it and reign.

James Adderley

Introduction

Every religious system either has political implications, or carries an explicit political theory. The Catholic variety of Anglicanism was no exception. In its most clearly articulated form it was connected via theological argument to a number of versions of what has come to be known as 'Christian socialism'. But it also had a conservative element, which was apparent in the formulations of the Oxford Fathers, and which has been seen since in the uncritical approach which treats anything labelled 'Catholic' as good and desirable, without regard to other issues.[1] There was also a positive support in some quarters for hierarchy, order, established authority and tradition, and a view of novel or independent thought as threatening. Anglo-Catholicism could be attractive to conservatives because it offered a security compounded of tradition, dogma, and the beauty and mystery of Catholic worship. The writings of T. S. Eliot are instructive here, especially *The Idea of a Christian Society*.

The social quietism of Christianity at the beginning of the nineteenth century has often been documented.[2] The widespread middle class fear of the masses following the French Revolution, and the rise of the radical movements, encouraged the belief (later to be endorsed by Marx) that the social

121

function of religion was to ensure stability and order. Either the poor were excluded from the churches, or they were relegated to the seats at the back where they would not offend the better-off churchgoers. They were taught to eschew the dangerous ideas of 'French philosophy' and to accept their place in society as divinely-ordained. As the much-quoted hymn by Mrs Alexander has it:

> The rich man in his castle,
> The poor man at his gate:
> God made them high and lowly,
> And ordered their estate.

Keble held views implying an endorsement of the existing social order. 'The rich and the poor meet together: they are (so to speak) correlatives in this great system of God Almighty's ordering; as parents and children are, and subjects and rulers, and servants and masters, and young and old: one cannot be without the other. Their mutual interests, and rights, and duties, fill up a large space indeed in this world of our trial: they are entwined and mingled in a thousand ways: they meet each other at every turn. This is God's ordinance. . . .'[3]

But there was also a striking, if limited, critique of some common religious assumptions, as John Orens has recently shown.[4] The Tractarians were shocked by the complacency apparent in the readiness of the clergy to attack the sins of the poor while ignoring those of the rich and powerful. Pusey, for example, compared the attitude of caring for the suffering shown by the primitive Church with the indifference of nineteenth century Christians. He claimed that the poor are the 'visible representatives' of Christ to the rich and yet the rich ignore him. Appealing for slum missions, he saw the need to 'grapple with our manufacturing system as the Apostles did with the slave system of the ancient world'.

Hurrell Froude attacked the view that the priesthood is an occupation for the middle classes, and advanced the cause of the poor. He developed the radical distinction between Church and state which Keble had drawn in his Assize sermon, suggesting that while the state is the preserve of the rich and powerful, the Church is the preserve of the poor.[5] Ward thought that the Church ought to be 'the poor man's court of justice' and strongly attacked its failure to stand up for the underprivileged. The 'ordinary condition' of the Church, he argued, should be 'one of opposition to those in worldly status'.

Such attitudes were partly derived from the old high church tradition. But fundamentally, and crucially for later developments, they were grounded in the Tractarians' stress on the Incarnation. This led to a qualified acceptance of humanity and the world, as opposed to Evangelical rejection of both based on the primacy attached to the doctrines of the Fall and the Atonement. Tractarians argued that the world itself has a sacramental quality, and that the Incarnation has given men high status. Wilberforce, in his book on incarnational doctrine, claimed that God became through Christ the representative and head of the whole human race, and that the bond between the human and the divine is permanent. Moreover, the social aspect of Christian life was strongly emphasized by the Tractarians. One becomes a Christian, Newman wrote, by being taken into the membership of the Church, and it is the means whereby the gifts of the Spirit are to be made available to the whole human race. Such a view was totally opposed to the Evangelical notion that the Church is a society of the chosen, of redeemed individuals.

Yet despite all these radical ideas, there was still a limit to the Tractarians' social theory. Charity and legislative reform were the means they advocated for dealing with social ills, and the hopes they had of these were limited – an end to suffering was not to be expected in this life. Christ had said that his kingdom was 'not of this world', and that rather ambiguous statement was given a conservative meaning by the Oxford Fathers despite their criticisms of the Victorian social order. Yet an alternative, and far more radical, reading is possible: that Christ's kingdom is not of the world as it is now, and that a social transformation is necessary to make the world worthy to enshrine it. This is the view which was to be advanced in various ways by the post-Tractarian generations, and to be put into practice by the slum ritualists of the later period.

Maurice and Headlam

'Christian socialism' was a term first employed in *Tracts on Christian Socialism* (1850), which came to refer to the body of ideas developed by Frederick Denison Maurice (1805-1872), Charles Kingsley (1819-1875) and J. M. Ludlow (1821-1911). As has often been suggested, it is a misleading term; the attitudes of Maurice and his associates are better described as 'Tory paternalist'.[6] Maurice is a bridge figure between the qualified criticism of the Tractarians and later developments. He was cautious, politically timid, anxious for the Church to follow a middle way of reconciliation between contending parties. He respected tradition, and saw the ideal state as monarchical, aristocratic and democratic, the ideal Church as both Catholic and Protestant, orthodox and liberal. His counterparts exist today, still preaching a *via media*, and still attracting accusations of woolliness and lack of realism.

Maurice began with the doctrine of the Incarnation. God through this act had joined the whole human race to himself; human nature was thereby glorified, and the bond thus created could not be broken. Here he differed from Pusey, who taught that post-baptismal sin would shatter the link. Maurice was particularly concerned about the implications of such teaching for the 'wretched creatures who spend eighteen hours out of twenty-four in close factories and bitter toil . . .' who are told 'that if they spent the remaining six in prayer – he need not add fasting – they may possibly be saved'.[7] To argue thus is to make their lot even more miserable.

The Church has a far more positive message for the poor. Every man and woman is made in the image of God. No sin, not even that of the Fall, can distance us from the concern of God as loving father, and since no one can resist the power of that love, the prospect of eternal torment is unthinkable. God is present in our midst now; his kingdom has already been established on earth, and it is here that his purposes are to be accomplished. He has ordained that the human race shall become a divine society; all social institutions from the family to the economic and political spheres are thereby made sacred. We are to live out the Christian life daily, in our mundane existence, in our relations with our neighbours. God's concern is for all humanity but especially, reversing the conventional order of priorities, for the poor, evidenced by his entry into 'the state of the lowest beggar, of the poorest, stupidest, wickedest wretch whom that Philosopher or that Pharisee can trample upon', in order to 'redeem the humanity which Philosophers, Pharisees, beggars, and harlots share together'.[8]

It was this type of social theology, linking together Tractarian incarnationalism and sacramentalism with a view of the kingdom of God as a present reality and not something confined to the remote world beyond death, which led Maurice to Christian socialism. If God's purposes are to be accomplished on earth, the present social order must be judged against divine standards, by which it is found wanting. Thus theology is emancipated from subjugation to the contemporary fashions of economic individualism, and its autonomy as a source of social standards is asserted. (The lessons for today should be obvious here.) According to Maurice it is not enough to say that suffering and injustice must be endured; they must be abolished. All men and women, not merely the affluent, must be able to enjoy a full life. Co-operation must replace competition.

But how was this to be done? What was the 'Christian social-ism' of which he spoke, and which Marx was to condemn virulently as 'but the holy water with which the priest con-secrates the heart-burnings of the aristocrat?'[9] About practical proposals, Maurice had little to say, and the few policies he suggested were constrained by his conservatism: he was in favour of trade unions and co-operative workshops, but was also a stout defender of the monarchy and the institution of private property, and opposed universal suffrage. Though he had once called himself a Chartist, and his movement had arisen partly as a response to Chartism, he volunteered to be a special constable in 1848 to help deal with the expected Chartist uprising. He had no general programme of social reform. Thus his significance for the development of Christian socialism was an important, if limited, theoretical develop-ment: he forged a link between certain key elements of the movement's theological base, and set out a powerful critique of Victorian assumptions. But later writers were to go much further.

By the 1860s the generation of slum clergy had begun to affect their parishes, not only through ritual strife but also through their attempts to cope with the social problems which surrounded them. Both Mackonochie at St Alban's, Holborn and Lowder at St Peter's, London Docks rapidly encountered widespread poverty, ill-health and exploitation among their parishioners.[10] But their response was limited, and Davies has recently suggested that it was handicapped by class-based perspectives. Their work was largely at the level of charity and individualistic protest. The assumptions from which some started are illustrated in the following appeal by W. J. E. Bennett of St Barnabas', Pimlico: 'Come with me into the lanes and streets of this great city. Come with me and visit the dens of infamy, and the haunts of vice, ignorance, filth and atheism, with which it abounds. Come with me and read the story of Dives and Lazarus. . . . Then look at your noble houses, and the trappings of your equipages, the gold that glitters on your side-boards, and the jewels that gleam on your bosoms; then say within your secret conscience, as standing before the great and terrible God at the day of judgement, What shall I do if I give not of the one, to relieve the other?'[11] There is no suggestion here of any fault in the social order, only an appeal for the charity of the rich.

Although Father Stanton described himself as 'politically socialistic' and Mother Kate, of St Saviour's, Priory, Haggerston, called him a 'revolutionary', his attitudes are better classified as liberal. Indeed, it may well have been the strong conservatism of the clergy house at St Alban's, Holborn, which led him to appear extreme.[12] Moreover, Davies has argued, his model of class relations was one of deference, and towards the end of his life he displayed a sentimental advocacy of pietistic acceptance of one's place in life not very different from that of Mrs Alexander's hymn. Whether one accepts all Davies' criticisms or not, it is certainly true that the understanding of the causes of social problems and their solution found among Catholic clergy at that time was very limited – as it still is.[13]

This was not true of all, however, and one notable exception was Stewart Headlam (1847-1924). Headlam was educated at Eton and Trinity College Cambridge. He was ordained to a curacy at St John's, Drury Lane, in 1870, and moved to Bethnal Green in 1873. Here in 1877 he founded the Guild of St Matthew which was to become a small but influential group engaged in the linkage of religious and political ideas and activities, employing what Maurice Reckitt has called 'shock tactics' and 'revolutionary defiance'. The GSM was always relatively small in numbers, reaching a peak in the 1890s, when there were 99 clergy members and 265 laymen. It lasted for thirty-two years until Headlam dissolved it in 1909. He is often seen as little more than an eccentric failure, and any brief outline of his career, a good part of his life outside the parochial ministry, and involving conflicts over socialism, sacramentalism, secularism, devotion to our Lady and music hall ballerinas, makes it easy to see why, but Orens has argued that this is a considerable underestimate.[14] Drawing on the ideas of Maurice, whose influence on him was very great, Headlam formulated an understanding of the connection between Catholicism and social and political action far more radical than that of his predecessors, and the causes for which he campaigned were all part of this understanding.

Headlam opposed theological liberalism because he thought it led to the undermining and watering down of Christian teaching on social justice. He had his own distinctive interpretations of the sacraments. Baptism is open to everyone: it is inclusive and democratic since if we are the children of one Father, we must all be brothers. The Church is a society of equals, a socialistic society, at its head the revolutionary from Nazareth. Headlam criticized the excessive supernaturalism of Tractarian attitudes to the Eucharist, and saw such other worldliness as a major obstacle to the improvement of social conditions.

Headlam's politics are an expression of his theology. He remained a political Liberal, and his proposals for economic reform were strongly influenced by Henry George's idea of a single tax. Yet at the same time he believed in the socialization of capital and land. There seems to be a contradiction between his support for the ideas of the American prophet of laissez-faire and such socialistic proposals. According to Orens this can be resolved by grasping that Headlam was attracted by George's vision of a future age 'of unrivalled beauty, joy and plenty; an age in which man's creative power, shackled so long by poverty and oppression, would build a new world in accordance with the divine plan'.[15] He also feared the establishment of a future socialist tyranny as horrible as that of the landlord and the capitalist. In his opinion true socialism aims at 'the greatest possible economic change with the least possible interference with private life and liberty. Spurious socialism, on the other hand, postpones the initiation of those reforms which are necessary to bring about the economic changes, but interferes with the individual in every possible way; and especially does it take delight to interfere with the pleasures and morals of the individual.'[16]

Headlam thus opposed the tendency to bureaucratic collectivism already apparent within the Fabians. He also rejected the politics of the ILP, which he called 'insufficiently socialist'. His vision was of a socialism which was not tied to the interests of a particular class but which had a much wider constituency. The ILP was uninterested in the poorest classes – women, the unskilled, agricultural labourers. Also it saw itself as representing labourers while defining them inadequately – to Headlam, teachers, civil servants and clergymen came into this category as much as industrial workers. Headlam's vision was thus broader and more sophisticated than that of many of his peers.

Fundamentally he was not interested in a 'socialist party for churchmen', but in a vision of the kingdom made apparent in the Mass. This led him to the notorious controversy over music hall ballerinas, in which he compared the grace of the ballerina to that of Christ, leading to contemporary supposition that he was mad. But Headlam, knowing full well that the music hall was the site of vice and corruption, also saw it as a source of the 'beauty, and joy, and pleasure' so much lacking in the lives of ordinary people, whose problems were not to be solved merely by economic means. In this sense he was an advocate of 'art for the people' which they enjoyed, not merely for their 'improvement'. Also in the beauty of the ballet he saw a sign of the kingdom of God. Dancing is an 'eighth sacrament'; 'the poetry of motion is the expression of unseen spiritual grace'. At the time this may well have seemed ridiculous; today perhaps it would be more acceptable.

Headlam can be faulted in a number of respects. His economics was naïve and he was excessively contentious. In his relations with members of his Guild of St Matthew he was dictatorial. He writes at times as if the kingdom of God will come through the actions of the Church alone, saying little about divine intervention. His treatment of scripture and his use of written authorities were dubious. Finally, his claim that Catholicism is the only guarantee of sound revolutionary politics seems absurd when one considers how reactionary many devout Catholics were and are.

The core of Headlam's faith is very different from that of the Tractarians. For him Catholicism is not adherence to ecclesial norms, but action based on a grasp of the symbolic meanings contained in creed and sacrament. Despite his oddities he is a strikingly modern and impressive figure.

From the Christian Social Union to the Catholic Crusade

Within a period of approximately thirty years around the turn of the century, a number of Anglican groups committed to some version of socialism were formed. The extent to which their socialism would have been recognized by secular socialists is debatable, and what they called socialism was varied in its content, but they represent further attempts to explore and work out in practice the implications of the new social theology.

The first of these, the Christian Social Union, was according to Norman [17] 'central, respectable and vague', and thus very different from the Guild of St Matthew, although the two memberships overlapped to some extent; for example Percy

Dearmer belonged to both. The CSU was not even formally committed to socialist ideas, and never had any working class members, although it achieved a membership of about 6,000, fifteen times that of the GSM. Nor was it connected with any political party or group, whereas the GSM had ties with the Fabians.

The CSU had emerged out of the 'Holy Party', a group founded in Oxford in 1875 to discuss liberal Catholic theology. Its leading figures were Gore, Scott Holland, Illingworth and Westcott, all influential in the Church and of upper middle class academic backgrounds, all greatly influenced by the philosopher T. H. Green. They were to produce the controversial essays entitled *Lux Mundi*, and to provide a focus for the social concerns of moderate Anglicans. As Orens tartly observes, 'Bishops and academics flocked to the union precisely because it gave them an opportunity to show their concern for the poor without requiring that they do very much about it'. Their highly academic approach provoked sarcasm from the GSM. ' "Here's a glaring social evil", they would announce mockingly, "let's read a paper about it." '[18]

Edward Norman calls Westcott a Chamberlain-style Liberal rather than a socialist, and regards his theoretical formulation of 'socialism' as opposed to 'individualism', on which he based his critique of the assumptions of political economy, as crude and unsubtle. The central principle which he advocated was co-operation between the various groups in society on some sort of organic model, and socialist Christians were to act as 'missionaries' for such ideas among politicians and employers. Socialist ideas would slowly permeate the social order and transform it. But he had little sense of the structural obstacles to such a process, nor any notion that collective action by the state might be necessary to achieve it; there was no analysis of the cultural impediments presented by what Marx called 'false consciousness' or what Gramsci was later to call 'class hegemony', nor of the necessity for the redistribution of wealth and power through the overthrow of class society. Westcott's influence seems to have derived more from his personality – another illustration of the role of charisma in the Catholic movement – which caused followers to feel 'lifted, kindled, transformed; we pledged ourselves, we committed ourselves; we were ready to die for the cause; but if you asked us why, and for what, we could not tell you'.[19]

The CSU was highly influential within the British churches: the Catholics, Quakers and Methodists were later to found their own Social Unions on similar lines. Once again an incarnational theology was employed to argue the need to be concerned with worldly matters and to strive for social justice. It was suggested that for the first time Christian principles were being applied to industry and politics (which was of course not the case), and Westcott was to claim in 1898 that there had been a gradual acceptance of the 'master-thoughts' of corporate obligation and corporate interdependence, so that it was now 'universally acknowledged among Englishmen that we all belong to one body, in which the least member has his proper function'.[20] No doubt Westcott intended to convey the worth of that 'least member', but the tone is highly paternalistic. Moreover, the substantive claim is simply absurd, especially since class antagonism was notably intense in the 1890s,[21] and suggests the remoteness of the speaker from the society in which he lived.

The action undertaken by the CSU included the preparation of a 'white list' of employers paying low wages, which led to a small-scale boycott and achieved some publicity for the cause. Various kinds of 'morally-guided' action were also advocated, such as frugal living by the rich to reduce social tension, and thoughtful investment of one's money. (This shows remarkable optimism about human nature and recalls the rule of CR, in the foundation of which Gore was a leader, that monks should retain their capital!) There was no consistent line over international issues such as the Boer War, which Westcott supported and Scott Holland and Gore opposed.

It is thus easy to suggest that indeed the CSU was little more than the upper middle class debating group which Marx had attacked and the GSM had caricatured. On this view a number of comments can be made. H. D. A. Major, assessing the results of Gore's labours for Christian socialism, suggested that the Church of England was transformed: 'She who had been aptly described as the Conservative party at prayer, became, as the result of Gore's influence, at least in the persons of her Anglo-Catholic clergy, the Socialist party at Mass.'[22] This famous and much repeated quotation is far too sanguine, but some more balanced conclusions are possible. The CSU was important, according to Jones[23] because of its influence on the Church's social thought, and its support for parliamentary action through reforming legislation. Orens notes the sophisticated presentation of an incarnational social policy. Leech[24] sees its importance firstly in the reforms which it achieved, and secondly in the establishment of a theological framework, especially by Gore, in which socialist thought could develop. *Lux Mundi*, Leech says, had an importance for Christian socialism comparable to that of *Fabian Essays* for British socialism as a whole.

Dissatisfaction emerged within the CSU after the general election of 1906 at which fifty-three Labour and Lib-Lab members were returned to Parliament. Inspired by this, the Church Socialist League was formed under the leadership of Lewis Donaldson, W. E. Moll, Conrad Noel and Percy Widdrington, with Mirfield, where Gore's ideas had influenced thinkers such as Samuel Healy, Neville Figgis and Paul Bull, as an important centre. The first president was the Revd Algernon West, who came not from the usual upper middle class background but from lower middle class origins. Once again this was a clerical movement, of the younger generation of clergy, critical of the middle class paternalism of earlier groups and of their failure to attract many working class members. The CSL sought to break with this approach and to draw closer to secular political movements. The general aim was a 'democratic commonwealth' with collective ownership of land and capital, to be used for the good of all. The essential parts of socialism were seen as 'necessary inferences' from the Christian faith: 'pity for the weak, justice for the oppressed, the inviolable sanctity of every individual life as an end in itself, and fellowship instead of competition as the dominant method in industry and commerce . . .'[25] There was of course a direct continuity in this formulation with those of earlier groups.

By 1910 there were 1,200 members, and by 1912 the group was actively involved in the industrial unrest of that year, with members including A. J. Penty, Maurice Reckitt and R. H. Tawney. It petitioned the Convocation of Canterbury that 'private ownership of land and capital should forthwith be made to cease'.[26] However, despite this 'activism', the CSL rapidly foundered on internal disputes. The new approach concealed divisions over the primacy of either theological or political action which soon became apparent. In 1912, under the influence of Percy Widdrington, the CSL opted for theology and the development of a 'Christian sociology' (by which was meant what nowadays would be called a 'social philosophy'). But the divisions between Widdrington and Noel especially were clear, and in 1916 Noel left the CSL, forming the Catholic Crusade two years later.

Widdrington saw the main work of the CSL as 'the conversion of church people', and a movement away from the tendency shown when, 'in the first years of the League's existence, in our eagerness to demonstrate our faith in the ideas latent in the Labour Movement, we came perilously near to becoming a political society. . . . Our concern with our fellow Churchmen is not to compel them to join a political party, but to accept the social implications of the Faith. . . .'[27] He was also worried about the possibility that unless the working classes roused themselves, state socialism would come.

The theories which all the CSL leaders except Noel adopted after 1914 were those of guild socialism. The medieval ideal which had been so influential on the spiritual development of the Catholic revival now became of great significance in its social thought. The goal was 'the return of Christendom' (the title of a collection of essays published in 1922), and Christendom was seen as involving a type of pluralism: a universal society containing a diversity of vocation.[28] According to Tawney it also possessed a moral order opposed to divisive individualism.

The CSL theorists wished to create the conditions under which such a morality might flourish again. Father Neville Figgis was one of the most influential writers here, advocating a 'community of communities' comprising the state, with the Church as a separate spiritual society. To achieve this there must be a transformation of the nature of civil society. Social change is to be brought about through acting upon society's moral standards by gradual permeation – again an idea which had appeared before, and which is hard to justify in the light of experience.

Maurice Reckitt, apart from being the best-known historian of the Anglican social movement, was another theorist of guild socialism. He advocated the modification of the sovereignty of the state, self-government in industry and the abolition of the wage system. The workers should have control over each industry, in partnership with the state, which would be the owner of the means of production. Reckitt distrusted state socialism as much as Widdrington. Like Widdrington he argued that it was necessary to develop a 'Christian sociology' as a basis for criticizing the drift towards bureaucratic collectivism, and for suggesting an alternative pattern of change.

All these ideas were brought together in *The Return of Christendom*. Industrial society was spiritually sick, based on a destructive and false individualism, and production and profit as ends in themselves rather than for any more ultimate goal.

Pride in work and craftsmanship were being destroyed, and neither communism nor secular socialism offered an adequate solution. But an alternative model existed in the medieval idea of Christendom. Nor was this retreat into a dream of the past; Christendom was directly opposed to the evils of modern capitalism, and it would have to fight them on the basis of what Widdrington called 'the regulative principle of theology'. The Church must become 'aflame with the faith of the Kingdom'; it will then challenge the forces of the modern industrial world as it challenged those of Roman imperialism. This will involve a revolution in thought comparable to that of the Reformation.[29]

On such a basis the League of the Kingdom of God was founded in 1923. Members were involved in the Anglo-Catholic Summer School of Sociology which was established in 1924 under the sponsorship of the Anglo-Catholic Congress, following Frank Weston's famous speech at the 1923 Congress in which he linked the 'worship of Jesus in the Tabernacle' with 'pity for Jesus in the slums'. From 1931 the journal *Christendom* was published under Widdrington's editorship. According to one member, 'what was begun was in fact a revolution; a return to social thinking upon the basis of theology which has resulted in the establishment of a definite and recognized school of thought the influence of which has been far wider than the extent of its own immediate circle of adherents, and the effects of which have been sufficiently described in the phrase "from ethics to sociology". . . . The claim which the Christendom Group has consistently made, that theology is the one reintegrating force precisely because it provides the world with a vision of itself from outside itself, providing men with a philosophy of ends and means, and thus a true hierarchy, has amounted to a liberation and enlargement of our social thought.'[30]

On the other hand, it has been said of the Christendom Group that while they combined 'brilliance of intellect and imaginative grasp of problems' they were also 'unhampered by any solid knowledge of the realities of the issues with which they tried to grapple, and any willingness to learn from experts. As a result they naturally failed to say anything of significance on economic matters.'[31] The influence of the 'social credit' theories of Major C. H. Douglas has also been criticized, though in fact the group was not exclusively committed to such theories.

Widdrington and his colleagues proposed a revolution by

tradition comparable to that of the Tractarians: the use of the past to change both present and future. Their employment of medievalism as a model for change seems to be condemned automatically these days, though why it should be is not clear. Such dismissals are often too glib: a label is not an argument. Medievalism is implicit in a number of other twentieth century ideologies which idealize the organic community. The Christendom Group's stress on the primacy of theology is perfectly legitimate for a church-based group, and they worked out in great detail the radical implications of such an approach. Moreover they were also correct to contend that an economic revolution is pointless if it is not associated with moral change. Finally, their critique of technological society was original in its day, and has been widely adopted since.

When Conrad Noel founded the Catholic Crusade in 1918, he was already following a different route from Widdrington (although they were in fact neighbours in rural Essex parishes). Noel thought that a social revolution must be founded on what he called 'the whole Catholic religion', and criticized the CSL for admitting members who were not Catholic and who held theological doctrines which were the equivalent of capitalist individualism. From his arrival as Vicar of Thaxted in 1910, he set about the transformation of parish life, both through the introduction of Catholic worship and through the teaching of socialism; in 1918 he formed the Crusade, whose aim was 'to transform the Kingdoms of the world into the Commonwealth of God' through Catholic socialism.

Noel had been greatly influenced by the ideas of Stewart Headlam, and, like him, believed that the showing forth of socialist principles was inherent in the liturgy. I have described elsewhere the Corpus Christi ceremonies at Thaxted, which Noel saw as 'the procession of the Divine Outlaw'. The power of symbols to evoke high emotions was vividly illustrated here. Noel's ritual, as expressed in his notion of the 'Red Mass', the significance of Benediction and the procession of the Host, was in part a political drama of symbolic protest. According to him, ritual was subversive. 'We preach the Christ Who all through His life stressed the value of the common meal, the bread and wine joyously shared among His people, the Mass as prelude to the New World Order in which all would be justly produced and equally distributed. . . . But all this involves politics, and we are often rebuked for mixing politics with religion. Well! the blind following of any political party, the politics of the party hack, these are certainly not the business of the pulpit; but politics, in the wider sense of social justice, are part and parcel of the Gospel of Christ, and to ignore them is to be false to His teaching.'[32]

Another symbolic conflict took place in 1921, the so-called 'battle of the flags'. This was over the display in Thaxted Church of the Sinn Fein tricolour and the red flag of international socialism. Noel objected to the Union Jack, which he saw as 'the modern flag of brute force dominion', in contrast to the flag of St George which symbolized 'just dealing and freedom'. Opponents of Noel, supported by new inhabitants of the village who moved in after the war, attempted to get these flags removed. Noel resisted, and a struggle took place both legally in the consistory court and physically in Thaxted church, when Cambridge undergraduates broke into the church and pulled the flags down. Eventually the flags were removed by court order.

From its beginnings in 1918, the Catholic Crusade was committed to what it saw as the whole Catholic faith, involving revolution and the establishment, by force if necessary, of 'a classless cooperative society on communist lines'. A leaflet encouraged would-be members to 'Help the Catholic Crusade to shatter the British Empire and all Empires to bits . . .'. Noel's theology was grounded in the doctrine of the Incarnation and in the sacraments. It gave rise to a philosophy which was relevant to the whole of life: 'it will change your views on music, on decoration, on the colour of a piece of material, equally with your views of man's end, the reading of history and the revolution'.[33] Noel was to echo Headlam in suggesting that 'Every wayside flower is a sacrament of His body and blood . . . God is manifest in splendid men and women' and 'every human heroism is a Revelation'. God is imminent, perpetually active in the world, but was also fully incarnate in 'Jesus, the Christ, His Only Son, Our Lord, wholly God and wholly Man, conceived by the Holy Ghost, born of the Virgin Mary . . . who rejoices that her Son is casting down the mighty from their thrones and exalting them of low degree . . .'.[34]

Noel was an eclectic and idiosyncratic thinker, despite his putative Catholicism. His contribution to Catholic socialism lies in his radical democracy: the Holy Spirit is present in all people; all are priests, not just the ordained or believers; the Holy Spirit is continuously present to inspire and guide. Politically he saw the achievement of the kingdom as an immediate task. These views led him to move increasingly to the left. Eventually he was to become a Leninist and Stalinist, and it was as the conflicts thus aroused that the Catholic Crusade foundered. Father John Groser and the group based at Christ Church, Watney Street, were 'driven out' according to Reg Groves, in 1932, and the Crusade collapsed in 1937. It had always been a small group – membership never reached 200,[35] partly because of the control exercised over entry, but largely because 'it could create its groups and common life only around a parish church conducted by a Crusade priest'.[36] In other words it seems to have been as clericalized as any other Catholic group, and was dominated by Noel in much the same way as Headlam had dominated the GSM. There was no scope for variety of opinion over the political conflicts of the 1930s. The Order of the Church Militant which Noel founded to take its place had only a short life, and died with him in 1942.

Catholic socialism today

After the collapse of the Crusade, Catholic socialism was in the doldrums for a long time. Partly this was because it had inherent limitations: it was small in numbers, hampered by clericalism, and unable to exert much influence on secular political activity. Social concerns were transmitted more widely within the Church of England through the writings of leading figures like Archbishop William Temple. Finally, with the coming of the welfare state, it seemed as if the concerns of the Christian socialists had now been taken over by society as a whole.

The distinctively religious approach continued in the Society of Socialist Clergy and Ministers, led by Stanley Evans. Another group, the Socialist Christian League, whose president was R. H. Tawney, was linked to the Labour Party. A collection of essays entitled *Papers from the Lamb* had some influence on Christian socialist thought during the fifties, but generally the Christian left like its secular counterpart was in some disarray, brought about largely by the revelations of the 20th Congress of the Soviet Communist Party and the invasion of Hungary, events which were to have traumatic consequences for the British and other European Communist Parties, and to lead eventually to the emergence of the secular New Left in the 1960s.

This group began a powerful critique of the deficiencies of western capitalist societies in publications such as the *May Day Manifesto* (1968), for which the writings of academics such as John Westergaard, Ralph Miliband, Peter Townsend and E. P. Thompson provided the scholarly foundations. It was argued that contrary to popular belief the welfare state had neither eradicated poverty nor brought about a substantial reduction of inequalities of income, wealth and power in general. In the debate which followed the Anglican Catholic left was little heard. The tradition was continued to a limited extent by individuals like Jack Putterill, son-in-law of Conrad Noel and his successor as vicar of Thaxted, and by Fr Joe Williamson, who while hardly within the socialist tradition nonetheless issued some stirring denunciations of social conditions in the inner city. There were also a few small groups like the Society of the Catholic Commonwealth which combined Thomism and Marxism, and Christian anarchists. However, the most interesting response to current conditions came not from within Anglicanism but from the small, short-lived Roman Catholic 'Slant' group, whose periodical of that name provided in the late 1960s a heady, if sometimes confusing, brew of Marxism, Catholicism, cultural analysis heavily influenced by the writings of Raymond Williams, and attempts at a sociology of the parish.

In the 1970s a new Catholic socialist movement appeared. A leading figure in this was Fr Kenneth Leech, who as early as 1962 had published an article in the radical high church magazine *Prism* in which he set out a 'theology of rebellion' related to the involvement of Christians in CND. Leech was one of the very few advocates of a revival of the Catholic tradition of Noel and Headlam in the 1960s, and the Jubilee Group, founded in late 1974, was intended to work towards that end within a current context which was perceived as 'pseudo-Catholic ... increasingly pietistic and decadent ...', with '... an approach to Christian social action which was often vague in its theological foundations and merely reformist in its practice'.[37]

Leech summarized the principles of the Jubilee Group as follows. Firstly, it rejected theological liberalism and modernism, regarding the latter as 'revisionist', and instead was committed to Catholic orthodoxy, described as 'a revolutionary faith which challenges the structures of this world at every point'. Secondly, it rejected any sort of centralized organization, preferring decentralized local groups which set out to explore and develop ideas, and operating a kind of 'anti-copyright rule' which actively encourages the reproduction and re-issue of all its literature. Thirdly, it rejected a purely 'academic' approach in favour of the integration of theory and praxis, since many of its members were heavily committed to other activities–'busy parish priests in most cases'. Fourthly, it was concerned with thought rather than action–not because it wanted to substitute theology for action, but because a 'solid basis of contemplation and theological reflection' was necessary for that action to be effective. 'As Daniel Berrigan pointed out, it is the contemplative who is subversive of the unrighteous order, for he begins to see through its spurious claims, to unmask its illusions, and thus to undermine its foundations.'

In the ten years since its foundation the Jubilee Group has produced a great deal of literature: duplicated discussion papers, pamphlets, and a massive collection, *Essays Catholic and Radical* (1983). It has sponsored series of Lent lectures in London and Bristol and has commented on current issues in press releases and pamphlets. It has drawn upon well-known and less-known writers with mixed but often stimulating results. Among its contributors have been James Bentley, Peter Hebblethwaite, E. L. Mascall, David Nicholls and Rowan Williams, while Leech himself has been a prolific author of letters to the press, pamphlets and books on theological and social issues. His *True God* (1985) is an impressive example of his thought. Within boundaries set by 'Catholic orthodoxy' and a theological critique of capitalism,[38] the Jubilee Group has brought about a wide range of discussion and the movement has grown: in early 1985 the membership numbered about 400.[39]

Ultimately, as Widdrington and his colleagues saw, the issues involved in Catholic social theory and philosophy are theological, whatever else they may be. It would be surprising indeed if Christian theology led directly to the programme of any political party, but that has not been claimed by members of the Catholic left (who differ among themselves, of course; there is no one version of 'Christian socialism' as I have tried to make clear). Rather they have asserted that Christianity must lead to a concern with social justice, to 'solidarity with the poor' as contemporary jargon has it, to political commitment and political action. But it is in theological terms that the controversies must be worked out.

One danger of Christian political commitment is that it may lead to an introverted sectarianism–a religious version of the minute splinter groups of Left and Right which pursue their own versions of the true faith with little noticeable impact on contemporary social issues either nationally or internationally. Such groups are open to criticism, not only because they are irrelevant or ineffective, but because it can be argued that their raison d'etre is to satisfy their members' needs rather than to have any genuine political or social consequences.

A quite different danger is that the Christian confronted with a Babel of contending doctrines may choose to ignore them all and sink into political quietism. This can be justified as 'tending one's own garden', or dealing with what one can manage while not wasting energy on problems on which the individual can have little or no impact. It is a tempting position to adopt, especially in a world dominated by big power politics, but can in turn be criticized as evasive and selfish. Political choices are unavoidable if one is to live up to the moral demands of Christian commitment, but they are certainly not easy.

Ultimately the social implications of Christianity must be a matter of interpretation, and that interpretation will inevitably be affected (though not *determined*) by the views of the interpreters and the socially-given assumptions with which they operate. We are all constrained to some extent by our social setting. But this does not mean that Catholicism is infinitely plastic, that it can be assimilated to any political or economic doctrine. The reverse is true: Catholic orthodoxy provides a set of standards against which such doctrines are to be assessed. And it seems clear, however unpalatable this may be to some modern Catholics, that Catholic social thought, from the early centuries to the present day, is fundamentally opposed to many of the taken-for-granted assumptions of contemporary British political discourse.

9

Conclusions

Men may celebrate no second century of our movement if
we do not determine now to stand in social or in
doctrinal issues plainly upon our own ground, with a
message and a philosophy for the whole range of human
life, and a true order of ends and values, which men may
reject indeed, but the distinctive character of which they
can no longer mistake.

Maurice Reckitt

Catholicism and change

Anglican Catholicism is a religious protest movement which
has been tamed. It no longer possesses the passion and
impetus which gave it both notoriety and strength in the first
hundred years of its existence. A number of reasons can be
given for this. Movements are affected by the social context
within which they exist. Catholicism was not confined to
Britain of course – a large part of its influence has been abroad,
notably in Africa. But British society over the past 150 years
has become increasingly secular in certain specific senses. This
is *not* to say that religion *per se* is being rejected, or that the
'religious sense' is withering – there is considerable evidence to
the contrary – but that with few exceptions, *institutional* religion has suffered severe attrition, and has become increasingly
privatized and fragmented. Consequently any movement like
Anglican Catholicism which operates within an institutional
context automatically experiences the problems which result.

However, there is no immutable process by which institutional Churches inevitably die, as is sometimes thought. On
the contrary, the history of the English Church suggests a
striking resilience. Britain has never been a fully Christianized
country except in a purely nominal sense. Christianity has
always, so far as we can tell from the historical evidence, co-
existed with other beliefs and with a large measure of apathy

and indifference. But over long time intervals there appears to be a recurrent pattern of rise and fall, peak and trough. In the eighteenth century large parts of the country were effectively outside the influence of the Church – in itself a pattern similar to that found in the medieval period, the so-called 'ages of faith'. One hundred years later various religious revivals, including Tractarianism, had brought about a renewal of church life. Another century on, decline is again apparent. We should not glibly conclude that hundred year cycles occur, but there is a pattern.

Anglican Catholicism has in some respects followed the typical path of what Wallace has called a 'revitalization movement',[1] that is, a movement which attempts the conscious and organized reconstruction of a society (and we should remember that the implications of Anglo-Catholic beliefs were that extensive; they were not confined to what went on in churches). Methodism is another example of the same type. Such movements begin in critical opposition to the established order, which they attempt to change in the most fundamental and far-reaching manner. They are perfectionist, aiming at the total realization of their aims and quite unwilling to compromise. But they may change in the course of time, both in order to attract a larger body of support, *and* as a consequence of success in that aim. A range of adaptive strategies can be brought into play, including modification or reinterpretation of the original message and qualified acceptance of the status quo. Changes of this sort can be seen in the later history of the Catholic movement, as the doctrinal and liturgical extremism of the early years was replaced by gradual accommodation in a Church which itself had been substantially altered in a Catholic direction. Success brought about moderation.

Other social changes are important. The rise of bureaucracy is one factor which has affected the Catholic movement adversely. As Bryan Wilson observes, 'There can be few human activities on which rational planning, administrative co-ordination and the regulations of bureaucratic organization have such deleterious effects as religious movements.'[2] Bureaucracies concentrate power, and this, together with their stress on rationality, erodes spiritual values. Consequently they are a major secularizing element within contemporary Churches, which increasingly find themselves travelling along paths dictated by bureaucratic reasoning. Centralization undermines local autonomy, and promotes reorganizations leading to a bland, uncontroversial middle-of-the-road Anglicanism. The emergence of career structures within the new bureaucratic agencies further weakens the traditional parochial ministry. The demand that effective use be made of resources at the diocesan or national level is used to justify withdrawal of plant and manpower from areas which become progressively de-Christianized, creating a vicious circle to which, within the accepted framework of rationalizing assumptions, only further bureaucratic responses appear possible. Catholics have protested from time to time about the consequences of these processes, but on the whole, like church members in general, they have reluctantly accepted the trend.

The rise of bureaucracy is associated with routinization and the decline of charisma. In the early stages, revitalization movements are driven by the emotional and social energies generated by charismatic leaders. In time, as the movement becomes successful, such energies dim and charisma fades. The movement will either cease to exist, or will be continued through the replacement of individual charisma by formal organization. At this stage, however revolutionary the movement was at the outset, it may become increasingly conservative. Since it is now incorporated to some extent in the status quo, it has a stake in the survival of existing arrangements. But if it is also partly deviant within the larger society, it may adopt an isolated social role for itself which can be maintained by a loyal group of supporters.

The Catholic movement has taken both these routes. A moderate form of Catholicism, as expressed in the Parish Communion, now the principal service in a majority of churches, and the incorporation of Catholics within church organization at all levels of the hierarchy and bureaucracy have undoubtedly had homogenizing effects. To a large extent Catholics today are indistinguishable from adherents of other parties in many of their attitudes and assumptions; only on crucial issues such as abortion or the ordination of women does a distinctive party line emerge. Catholic teaching, even on such central themes as the doctrine of the real presence or the place of Mary, is given a subdued emphasis. At the same time a minority, who might be labelled 'extremists' in terms of current norms, do advance such causes within the setting of devotional societies and churches with 'full Catholic privileges', but it is doubtful if they are much heard outside. Similarly, the Catholic socialism which was so prominent in the late nineteenth and early twentieth centuries now receives little attention from the wider society, and tends to be submerged within a more general protest from a socially concerned Church (as in the furore over the miners' strike of 1984, or the recent 'inner city' disputes).

The negative effects of rationalization and routinization are only likely to be arrested by recognition of their consequences. There is a debate here for the whole Church which has as yet hardly begun. If we follow Weber's analysis, the trend to excessive rationalization, the 'iron cage' of bureaucracy, can be arrested by the emergence of charismatic leaders. This suggests that a new Catholic revival, in order to break through constraints which are partly self-imposed, requires a critical vision which can understand what is wrong, *and* a leadership to convey this vision to others. Both of these are at present in short supply.

Some further factors connected with Catholic decline in recent decades may be discussed in the light of an article by Alan Wilkinson, published in 1978.[3] Firstly he notes the importance of the post-conciliar changes in Roman Catholicism – until then a rock by which Anglican Catholics could steer their course. Since Wilkinson wrote his article, of course, John Paul II has partially reversed some of the effects of these changes, with the undoubted approval of a section of the Catholic movement. Clearly, for some Anglican Catholics at least, Rome is still the central reference point, as recent conversions suggest. But there have been other views, such as the conception of a distinctively English Catholicism with elements including theological liberalism and a liturgical approach based on the Sarum use. Some adherents of this view saw the post-conciliar changes in Rome as a move towards their own position. No doubt there is an element of religious chauvinism here, but a number of independent commentators have remarked – sometimes approvingly, sometimes not – on the 'Anglicanization' of the Roman Church.

Evangelicalism, Wilkinson says, is now 'more powerful, coherent, intelligent and self-confident than it has been for more than a century'. Catholicism has little influence on youth, since it has never had an adequate youth ministry of its own, and SCM, within which some Catholics worked, has now virtually destroyed itself. Perhaps his point might be slightly qualified: some Catholic churches have a large youth membership, especially the 'Catholic shrines' in the major cities, and in most churches there are some young people who are strongly committed to the Catholic cause. But they are often few in number, and have to maintain their commitment against the psychological pressures caused by the predominance of elderly women: as one respondent told me in somewhat brutal terms, 'to be a Catholic sometimes seems to involve membership of a female geriatric institution'.

Wilkinson notes that Anglo-Catholic congregationalism has been affected greatly by post-war population movements, and the Parish Communion has had levelling-down as well as levelling-up effects. I suggest that these two factors worked together. At the same time as structural changes in the wider society reduced, and in some cases decimated, congregations, the distinctive Catholic ethos was weakened by liturgical changes originally inspired by Catholic insights. But in the search for 'relevance' all too often the Catholic stress on mystery and holiness disappeared from sight, leaving nothing to give the young even an inkling of what had so captured previous generations. This is perhaps one reason why the new religious quest from the late 1960s onwards sometimes looked east for inspiration. Also, as Wilkinson says, the charismatic movement, which emphasizes unity through experience rather than through doctrine and structures, and which is legitimated for some Anglican Catholics by widespread Roman Catholic participation, has been 'another factor in the erosion of the distinctive coherence of Anglican Catholicism'.

Wilkinson also draws attention to two consequences of recent religious thought. Firstly he notes the growth of radical questioning in the 1960s, which involved many who in previous generations would have been 'rebels in the Anglo-Catholic cause', and which led to subsequent disillusion. The radicals, he says, found some of their ideas to be mistaken, and showed a lack of staying power in the face of entrenched conservatism. Secondly, there is a continuing suspicion of authority in 'the mood of the period', (the late 1970s), and this is expressed even in the view of the Doctrine Commission that 'Christian life is an adventure, a voyage of discovery, a journey, sustained by faith and hope . . .'. Wilkinson observes that this is not a very traditional Christian way of looking at truth; fashionable catch phrases which he mentions, such as 'playing it by ear', 'open-ended', 'doing your own thing', 'let's see how it turns out', or 'off the cuff', all suggest a leadership which is basically uncertain, and very much under the influence of liberalism and the 'cultured despisers' of religion. Such an approach is hardly likely to enthuse more than a small minority.

A return to a more conservative approach is sometimes advocated on the grounds that for many people life is already difficult enough without the public display of a lack of confidence by those to whom they turn for guidance and reassurance. There is an element of truth in this: an uncertain leadership does not inspire, and a Catholic equivalent of 'conviction politics' would attract a following. But to see this as the one true face of Anglican Catholicism would be highly misleading: as I have shown earlier, the liberal element in Catholic thought has been present from the early days of the movement. To ignore current scholarship and interpretation would be to create a cognitive ghetto, and this would merely add to the sectarian tendencies of a movement which is already remote in many respects from the world of the 1980s. To be renewed, Catholicism has to engage with that world at a number of levels, including the intellectual, and a constructively critical approach to both conservative and liberal dogma is possible for Christians with a strong spirituality who have grasped the radically subversive nature of their creed. Such an approach is not easy – it is frequently painful – but it may be unavoidable if one is to be intellectually alive.

The Catholic, Wilkinson says, should know the importance of ritual, role, mythology and symbolism in community life. He should be aware that religion, tradition and the Church are essential to both individual and communal faith, binding individuals to each other and to their past. Because of this awareness he ought to be more open than the Evangelical or liberal to the importance of what Towler has called 'common religion',[4] and to regret that because of its emphasis on good taste and culture, the Church of England fails to produce the 'vulgar' Christianity which was once found in the Anglo-Catholic slum parishes, dissenting chapels and Merseyside Roman Catholicism. In the memorable passage which I have already quoted in chapter 4, Wilkinson asks, 'Do not the Stations of the Cross, the Rosary, clouds of incense, votive candles, Benediction and being splashed with buckets of holy water stand for something in religion which the Liturgical Commission will never comprehend?' Here Wilkinson recalls a fundamental religious insight of the Catholic revival, put in a more general way by Bernard Walke fifty years before: 'ceremonial and drama ... music and painting ... (are) modes by which the soul of man becomes conscious of unseen realities'.

Above all, Wilkinson suggests, the Catholic will be oriented to that other world which for the believer gives meaning to this. Hence he will see sacramental confession as something which should not be abandoned in favour of the 'valuable but different' approaches of counselling and psychotherapy. And he will value the monastic tradition for its support of the eschatological dimension of human life, the reminder that its goal is only realized fully beyond this world. Other-worldliness in this sense, Wilkinson says, is not often spoken of in the Church of England today.

Priests and professionalism

Most clergy carry out their tasks from day to day conscientiously and with humanity. Unfortunately some do not; they are engaged in a self-created drama which gives meaning to their own lives while at the same time exploiting the laity who form their congregations as mere objects for their own gratification. Often they do not realize this and would be shocked if it were drawn to their attention. But anyone who has had contact with the Catholic movement is forced to suspect the motives of some clergy, mainly because their behaviour seems so at odds with the values for which they ostensibly stand.

Clergy experience other problems. Some have lost touch with the theology which should inspire them; it is not necessary to suppose that every priest should be an academic *manqué* to argue that some are out of touch with current controversies, lack intellectual curiosity, and either ignore contemporary debates or respond to them in tired and hackneyed terms. They sometimes appear to have read nothing (other than reports in 'party' periodicals or the *Church Times*) since leaving college. A minority are frightened by change and unable to cope with it, socially isolated, lonely, victims of physical or mental illness, imprisoned in sexual or marital problems, sometimes only managing to survive on alcohol. Pastoral care for such casualties by those in authority often seems minimal; indeed it is striking that for the clergy as a whole, basic 'repair work' is often not carried out, evidence of how remote can be the genuine practice of 'Christian community'.

One response of the clergy generally to a changing social climate has been the development of a 'professional' ethos. This is related to the growth of group and team ministries, the membership of committees, church and otherwise, with a variety of concerns often tenuously related to the priestly role, the establishment of relations with power and interest groups within a locality, and the production of vast amounts of paper-work. It is justified as the 'rational' use of limited resources, but the values associated with 'rationalism' are strongly hostile to the affective elements in the catholic ethos, and have greatly weakened it. By adopting such an approach Catholics (especially Catholic clergy) have accepted a modern form of 'worldliness', sometimes losing sight of the spiritual grounding of their work.

They have also forgotten the need to carry people along with them. Personal contact is an important means of con-veying the Catholic vision to others, but 'professionalism' leaves less time for visiting and other forms of socializing. In particular, the growth of a professional ethos partly counter-acts other factors making for reduced social distance between clergy and laity, and encourages clergy to regard members of parishes in the same way as social workers regard their populations – as 'clients'. There is an element of self-protection in this, but it works against the development of local com-munity. Christianity stresses that all Christians, regardless of status, are to be *friends*. John Macmurray says that 'The uniqueness of Christ's gospel is that it makes friendship the heart of life, the absolute to which all else is relative ... Christ's kingdom (is) the kingdom of friendship'.[5] This has not been understood by those clergy who appear to regard laity only as troublesome individuals necessary to provide congrega-tions and carry out mundane tasks, to be managed and manipulated in accordance with clerically-determined goals. I do not suggest that a majority of clergy are like this, but a sufficient number tend in such directions to justify drawing attention to them.

Finally, the continuing stress on the centrality of the priest reveals how the Catholic movement is still weakened by clericalism. Despite all the talk of the last twenty years, and despite the changes in the priest's role which I have discussed earlier, an active democratic involvement of all the laity is still remote.

Misogynism and homosexuality

There is a strong spirit of hostility to women among some sections within the Catholic movement, ironically since they are the major source of its support. This expresses itself particularly in opposition to women priests (though of course it is not the only reason for such opposition). In the backstage male world of the clergy house (a classically Goffmanesque setting), women (especially those most active within the congregation) are sometimes criticized and ridiculed in a remarkably unpleasant and un-Christian way. This may be accounted for both by the common gap between clergy and laity and by another factor already noted: misogynism is clearly linked in some cases to the homosexual element within the movement. I have mentioned this earlier in my discussion of the priestly role, but it requires further comment.

The homosexual issue is one on which Catholics need to reach a viable understanding which avoids the easy extremes of blind condemnation or bland indifference. The homosexuality of many male members of the movement, both priests and laity, and of some female members also, is the movement's 'open secret', widely recognized but little admitted. It gives rise to both moral and practical problems. The moral problems are associated with the traditional condemnation of homosexual practices as sinful. In recent decades total condemnation has been less supported, and confessors and other advisers dealing with such problems have tended to commend the establishment of settled relationships as preferable to casual sex. A number of well-known figures have 'come out', openly admitting their sexual orientation. Such changes have caused scandal among traditionally-inclined Catholics, while the more liberal have felt occasional unease at the outcome of the trend. Such an approach does not effectively cope with the casually promiscuous, and some fundamental questions arise about the extent to which Christian ethical principles are culturally relative. This is, of course, one aspect of the conservative/liberal dichotomy in modern Catholic thought.

The social aspects are also important. Homosexual cliques can be narrow, exclusive and malicious. (Of course they are not alone in this.) Also, as is well-known within the Anglo-Catholic sub-culture, certain theological colleges, societies and churches have the reputation of being homosexual enclaves. The extent to which this is true has never been clearly established, but concern is sometimes expressed that a movement which clearly has a strong gay element may become no more than that – not merely a sub-culture but a predominantly homosexual one. Were this to become a commonly-accepted image of the movement there is no doubt that Anglican Catholicism would be extensively, perhaps fatally, weakened in influence.

The future of Catholicism

The future of Anglican Catholicism is uncertain. It is shrinking, divided and ageing. The current weaknesses are deep within its culture and institutions and will not be changed by rhetoric alone. Even the recent movement for Catholic renewal has been seen by some participants as expressing the least attractive aspects of the Anglo-Catholic sub-culture: introversion, defensiveness, sexism, clericalism, misogynism, political management by an affluent élite, and failure to address a large number of contemporary theological and political issues. One writer has described it as displaying 'the classic symptoms of sectarianism: a really dangerous mixture of fear and complacency'.[6] Another contributor to the same collection suggests that for some elements in the movement '"authentic Catholicism" seems to be mostly about liturgy and how many bits from the Missal we can get in, about incense and vestments and buying clerical gear from Rome. In the end I fear most of all that "Catholic" just comes to mean a camp way of doing things, an entirely sectarian concept, no longer a prophetic call to the churches.'[7] Contemporary Anglican Catholicism *can* be as petty and trivial as these quotations suggest, a perfect illustration of the sociologist Robert Merton's description of ritualism as the substitution of means for ends. The dangers of such attitudes were foreseen at the beginning of the movement, both by its friends and its enemies. They replace the Catholic vision by a mere ceremonial fetishism.

One hundred and fifty years after its beginnings, Anglican Catholicism has run into some of the classic problems of the religious protest movement. It has become routinized and sclerotic: social change has removed large sections of its original constituency and it has failed to find a new one. Instead it rests feebly within a crumbling edifice, speaking largely to itself. The prophetic insights into the contemporary relevance of tradition which originally inspired it now sound empty through constant repetition. There are few leaders to give them contemporary freshness and appeal. The experience to which those insights gave rise is often absent from a liturgy impoverished by the slavish following of clerical fashion. The high view of human nature engendered by incarnationalism is now largely a cliché which has little impact on pastoral or social action. The introverted, sectarian, Anglo-Catholic sub-culture often repels an audience already diminished by advancing secularity.

Moreover it is little known or understood beyond that sub-culture, and its obscurity is sustained by the reluctance of Catholics to get involved in the kind of promotional activities which Evangelicals successfully operate. Catholic meetings are often poorly supported and dominated by unrepresentative minorities. The limited range of Catholic literature available is unattractive and expensive. Little is done to alter the negative view of Anglican Catholicism which is widely held by outsiders – for example, the term 'high church' is often used in a derogatory sense. The meaning of 'Catholic', the vision of life which it embodies, its sacral emphasis, the praxis by which it renews and sustains the sense of the sacred, all these are unknown to most people. For many, even regular churchgoers, religion is not at the centre of their lives, but is only, as W. S. F. Pickering says,[8] a 'leisure-time pursuit', or a boring duty half-heartedly undertaken.

The Catholic revolution begun in Oxford 150 years ago has faltered. But at a time when life for many people, haunted by the spectres of economic decline, social collapse and nuclear war, seems increasingly bleak and empty of meaning, the Catholic faith continues to offer an alternative hope. This hope was grasped and acted on by the Tractarians and their succes-sors with far-reaching results. It retains a similar potential today. But genuine renewal involves more than a defensive obsession with the trivia of liturgy, opposition to the ordina-tion of women or attacks on the latest liberal bishop, which merely confirm popular stereotypes of the essential remote-ness and irrelevance of religion. If this is all Anglican Catholicism amounts to, it will never be more than a sect, a visible contradiction of its claim to be 'Catholic'.

A new revolution by tradition is possible. In its heyday the strength of Anglo-Catholicism lay in its ability to bring back into a church made uncertain by the effects of social change a sense of the reality of the supernatural and of the presence of the sacred in everyday life. It was thus able to generate a high level of commitment, purpose and enthusiasm among its supporters; the elements of eccentricity which also existed were of no great importance – indeed were part of its charm. Catholicism in the parishes created institutions which pro-duced both local community – the other side of the much-criticized 'congregationalism' – and the sense of the numinous without which religion is constantly in danger of succumbing to the secular world. The movement has declined in part because both have become weakened.

Revolutions are made by people with a vision. To achieve genuine and enduring renewal Catholics must grasp what they have often carelessly thrown away. This involves a recovery of Catholic tradition at three levels: spiritual, liturgical and social. A critical Catholicism is needed, which because it is grounded in spirituality and in a liturgy which manifests the sacred, is unafraid to measure everything, including its own current beliefs and practices, against the standards of orthodox tradition. On this basis could be developed a genuine care for people, often seen in the past but now lacking in those clergy who have retreated from the world into the security of the study, the committee, the church bureaucracy, or ritual fetishism. Catholicism also needs to engage both theoretically and practically with socio-political issues, and here the tradition of Maurice, Headlam, Gore, Figgis, Widdrington, Noel and Groser, despite its limitations, offers the basis for a renewed vision. In all these ways a rich but neglected heritage is waiting to be drawn on.

References

1 Introduction

1 Hugh McLeod, *Class and Religion in the Late Victorian City*, Croom Helm 1974: 184.
2 A Congregational convert to Anglo-Catholicism, quoted by McLeod op. cit.: 248-49.
3 op. cit.: 249.
4 Peter L. Berger, Brigitte Berger and Hansfried Kellner, *The Homeless Mind*, Penguin 1974: 192-93.
5 Perhaps I should immediately add that this implies no judgements whatsoever as to where 'true' Catholicism is to be found, but is merely a convenient piece of shorthand; constant repetition of the longer terms rapidly becomes tedious. Nor do I wish to imply that Anglican Catholicism can be treated as a social unity – I argue just the opposite.

2 The Catholic Revolution

General Bibliography
A list of the main historical works (on events and ideas) covering the area may be useful. What follows is inevitably selective. I have found the following helpful and interesting – not always for the reasons intended by the author.

G. W. O. Addleshaw, *The High Church Tradition*, Faber, 1904; Peter F. Anson, *Building up the Waste Places*, Faith Press, 1973; W. L. Arnstein, *Protestant versus Catholic in Mid-Victorian England: Mr Newdegate and the Nuns*, University of Missouri Press, 1982; S. Baring-Gould, *The Church Revival*, Methuen, 1914; J. Bentley, *Ritualism and Politics in Victorian England: the Attempt to Legislate for Belief*, Oxford University Press, 1978; C. Booth, *Life and Labour of the People in London, third series: 'Religious Influences'*, 1902; D. Bowen, *The Idea of the Victorian Church*, 1968; Y. Brilioth, *The Anglican Revival: Studies in the Oxford Movement*, Longmans, 1925; Olive J. Brose, *Church and Parliament: the Reshaping of the Church of England 1828-1860*, Oxford University Press, 1959; C. K. F. Brown, *A History of the English Clergy 1800-1900*, Faith Press, 1953; S. C. Carpenter, *Church and People 1789-1889: a History of the Church of England from William Wilberforce to Lux Mundi*, SPCK, 1933; Owen

Chadwick, *The Mind of the Oxford Movement*, A & C Black, 1960; idem, *The Victorian Church, Parts 1 & 2*, A & C Black, 1966 and 1970; Alice Chandler, *A Dream of Order: the Medieval Ideal in 19th-century English Literature*, University of Nebraska Press, 1970; Raymond Chapman, *Faith and Revolt: Studies in the Literary Influence of the Oxford Movement*, Weidenfeld and Nicholson, 1971; R. W. Church, *The Oxford Movement: Twelve Years 1833-45*, Macmillan, 1891; J. Cox, *The English Churches in a Secular Society: Lambeth 1870-1930*, Oxford University Press, 1982; C. P. S. Clarke, *The Oxford Movement and After*, Mowbray, 1932; G. S. R. Kitson Clark, *The English Inheritance*, 1950; A. O. J. Cockshut ed., *Religious Controversies of the Nineteenth Century*, Methuen, 1966; F. W. Cornish, *History of the English Church in the Nineteenth Century*, 2 vols 1910; F. L. Cross, *The Oxford Movement and the Seventeenth Century*, 1933; M. A. Crowther, *Church Embattled: Religious Controversy in Mid-Victorian England*, David and Charles, 1970; C. M. Davies, *Orthodox London*, Tinsley, 1873; C. Dawson, *The Spirit of the Oxford Movement*, Sheed and Ward, 1933; G. E. de Mille, *The Catholic Movement in the American Episcopal Church*, second edition 1950; T. Dilworth-Harrison, *Everyman's Story of the Oxford Movement*, Mowbray, 1932; Marcus Donovan, *After the Tractarians*, Philip Allan, 1933; L. E. Elliott-Binns, *Religion in the Victorian Era*, Lutterworth, 1936; Harold Ellis, *The Hand of the Lord*, Mirfield Publications, 1958; G. Every, *The High Church Party*, 1956; Geoffrey Faber, *Oxford Apostles: a Character Study of the Oxford Movement*, Penguin edition 1954; A. M. Fairbairn, *Catholicism, Anglican and Roman*, 5th edition 1903; Eugene R. Fairweather ed., *The Oxford Movement*, Oxford University Press, 1964; J. R. Griffin, *The Oxford Movement: a Revision*, Christendom Publications, 1980; T. C. Hall, *The Social Meaning of Modern Religious Movements in England*, 1900; B. Heeney, *Mission to the Middle Classes*, SPCK, 1969; Anselm Hughes, *The Rivers of the Flood*, Faith Press, 1961; K. S. Inglis, *Churches and the Working Classes in Victorian England*, Routledge and Kegan Paul, 1963; A. C. Kelway, *The Story of the Catholic Revival*, Cope and Fenwick, 1915; E. A. Knox, *The Tractarian Movement 1833-1845*, 1933; W. L. Knox, *The Catholic Movement in the Church of England*, Philip Allan, 1923; idem and Alec R. Vidler, *The Development of Modern Catholicism*, Philip Allan, 1933; Roger Lloyd, *The Church of England in the Twentieth Century*, Longmans, 2 vols 1946 and 1950; idem, *The Church of England 1900-1965*, SCM, 1966; P. T. Marsh, *The Victorian Church in Decline: Archbishop Tait and the Church of England 1868-1882*, Routledge and Kegan Paul, 1969; J. Lewis May, *The Oxford Movement*, Bodley Head, 1933; idem, *The Unchanging Witness: Some Detached Reflections on the Oxford Movement and its Future*, Centenary Press, 1933; D. Morse-Boycott, *The Secret Story of the Oxford Movement*, Skeffington, 1933; R. Mudie-Smith, *The Religious Life of London*, Hodder, 1904; David Newsome, *The Parting of Friends: a Study of the Wilberforces and Henry Manning*, John

Murray, 1966; E. R. Norman, *Anti-Catholicism in Victorian England*, Allen and Unwin, 1968; idem, *Church and Society in England 1770-1970*, Oxford University Press, 1976; S. L. Ollard, *The Anglo-Catholic Revival*, Mowbray, 1925; idem, *The Oxford Movement and After*, 1932; idem, *A Short History of the Oxford Movement*, Mowbray, 1915; J. H. Overton, *The Anglican Revival*, 1897; idem, *The English Church in the Nineteenth Century 1800-33*, 1894; W. Palmer, *A Narrative of Events Connected with the Publication of Tracts for the Times*, Rivington, 1883; W. Perry, *The Oxford Movement in Scotland*, 1933; B. M. G. Reardon, *Religious Thought in the Nineteenth Century*, Cambridge University Press, 1975; idem, *Religious Thought in the Victorian Age*, Longman, 1980; G. Rowell, *The Vision Glorious: Themes and Personalities of the Catholic Revival in Anglicanism*, Oxford University Press, 1983; idem et al., *The Catholic Revival in Nineteenth Century Anglicanism*, J. Clarke, 1983; W. J. Sparrow Simpson, *The History of the Catholic Revival from 1845*, Allen and Unwin, 1932; R. A. Soloway, *Prelates and People: Ecclesiastical Social Thought in England 1783-1852*, Routledge and Kegan Paul, 1969; H. L. Stewart, *A Century of Anglo-Catholicism*, Dent, 1929; A. Symondson ed., *The Victorian Crisis of Faith*, SPCK, 1970; W. Prescott Upton, *The Churchman's History of the Oxford Movement*, Church Book Room, 1933; A. Vidler, *The Church in an Age of Revolution*, Penguin, 1965; W. A. Visser T. Hooft, *Anglo-Catholicism and Orthodoxy: a Protestant View*, SCM, 1933; Dieter Voll, *Catholic Evangelicalism*, Faith Press 1963; George Wakeling, *The Oxford Church Movement*, 1895; Walter Walsh, *The Secret History of the Oxford Movement*, Church Association, 1898; C. C. J. Webb, *Religious Thought in the Oxford Movement*, SPCK, 1928; J. F. White, *The Cambridge Movement: the Ecclesiologists and the Gothic Revival*, Cambridge University Press, 1962; John Wilkinson ed., *Catholic Anglicans Today*, Darton Longman and Todd, 1968; N. Yates, *Kent and the Oxford Movement: selected documents*, Allen Sutton, 1983; idem, *The Oxford Movement and Anglican Ritualism*, Historical Association, 1983.

Notes

1   K. A. Thompson, *The organizational response of the Church of England to social change*, Oxford D. Phil. 1967: vii.
2   Anthony Russell, *The Clerical Profession*, Blackwell, 1984.
3   Alice Chandler, *A Dream of Order: the Medieval Ideal in Nineteenth Century English Literature*, University of Nebraska Press, 1970.
4   op. cit. 11, 248.
5   Geoffrey Faber, *Oxford Apostles*, 1954 edn.: 332.
6   J. Embry, *The Catholic Movement and the SSC*, Faith Press, 1931: x.
7   Anthony Russell, op. cit: 106, my main source here is Russell's account of developments.
8   Peter F. Anson, 'The evolution of Anglo-Catholic ritual and cere-

monial 1830-1860', *Catholic Standard for Anglicans*, January 1966: 5. Further detail is given in 'The evolution of Anglo-Catholic ritual and ceremonial 1855-1868', *Catholic Standard for Anglicans* May 1966, 4-5. But cf. Marcus Donovan, *After the Tractarians* 1933, who claims that by the 1850s nine or ten London churches used vestments and four had introduced incense.

9 Quoted from Blomfield's *Charge to the Clergy* in that year.
10 Liddon, *Life of Pusey*: ii, 140.
11 D. Morse-Boycott, *Secret Story of the Oxford Movement*, Skeffington, 1933: 156.
12 Roger Lloyd, *The Church of England 1900-1965*, SCM, 1966: 121.
13 A. C. Kelway, *The Story of the Catholic Revival*, Philip Allan, 1933.
14 *Report of the Oxford Movement Centenary Congress, July 1933*, Catholic Literature Association: xiii.
15 *Congress Report* p. vii.
16 See e.g. Hugh Ross Williamson, *The Walled Garden*, 1956.
17 R. F. Littledale, *Innovations*, Mowbray, 1868: 4-5; quoted Hill 1973: 101.
18 Michael Hill, *The Religious Order*, Heinemann, 1973, chapters 4 and 5, the main source for this section.
19 Max Weber, *The Theory of Social and Economic Organization*, Free Press, 1964: especially pages 301, 313, 314.
20 Hill op. cit. 88.
21 And of course there are other groups with different 'charters', for example liberal and broad church, which to some extent crosscut the Catholic and Protestant groupings.
22 Hill op. cit. 109.
23 A. M. Allchin, *George William Herbert. Some Aspects of his Teaching*, Convent of the Holy Name, Malvern, nd.: 11; quoted Hill 1973: 124.
24 Max Weber, *The Theory of Social and Economic Organization*, Free Press, 1964: 358-59.
25 For a presentation of Pusey as hero, see Ollard, *The Anglo-Catholic Revival*: 91-93. The description of Wainwright comes from Darby 1966: 43 (see note 26). There is a splendidly laudatory account of Mother Emily (of the Sisters of the Church) in *A Valiant Victorian*, Mowbray, 1964, especially Chapter XI and p. 222.
26 See for example the *Centenary Book of the Church of the Annunciation, Brighton*, 1964; Joyce Coombs, *One Hundred Years on the Hill: St Peter's Streatham 1870-1970*; *The Story of St Margaret with St Columba, Leytonstone*, 1967; Madge Darby, *The First Hundred Years at St Peter's, London Docks*, 1966; Joyce Coombs, *One Aim: Edward Stuart 1820-1877*, 1975 (of St Mary Magdalene, Munster Square, London); Maud A. Morgan, *Father Eves of St Alban's, Holborn*, SPCK, 1956.

27   Weber op. cit. 364.
28   Hill op. cit. 1973: 131.
29   Article XXVI of the Articles of Religion in the Book of Common Prayer.
30   John Gunstone, 'Catholics in the Church of England': 189-91, in John Wilkinson ed., *Catholic Anglicans Today*, Darton, Longman and Todd, 1968.
31   Joachim Wach, *Sociology of Religion*, University of Chicago Press, 1944: 173-186.

3 The meaning of 'Catholicism'

1   Palmer: *A Narrative of Events* 1883 ed.: 99f.
2   A. R. Vidler, *The Church in an Age of Revolution*, Penguin, 1965: 51.
3   Keble, quoted Chadwick ed., *The Mind of the Oxford Movement*, 1963: 39.
4   In Tracts 38 and 41 (1834), and in *Lectures on the Prophetical Office of the Church* (1837).
5   Keble: *On Eucharistic Adoration* 1-2, 70.
6   Raymond Chapman, *The Victorian Debate*, Weidenfeld and Nicholson, 1968: 270.
7   Don Cupitt, *The Sea of Faith*, 1984: 80ff.
8   'Orders in the Church of England' in *Report of the Church Congress of 1889*: 302.
9   *Catholicism and Roman Catholicism*: 1.
10   *The Idea of a Catholic Church*: 425.
11   *The New Theology and the Old Religion*: 159-60.
12   Letter to the *Church Times*, 22 December 1922: 3.
13   *The Church in the Twentieth Century*: 409.
14   'Problems and perils', *Church Times*, 5 October 1928.
15   James Carpenter: *Gore: a Study in Liberal Catholic Thought*, Faith Press, 1960.
16   Edward Gordon Selwyn ed., *Essays Catholic and Critical*, 3rd edition 1934: 115.
17   op. cit. 340.
18   This discussion draws extensively on John R. Orens, *The Mass, the Masses and the Music Hall: Stewart Headlam's Radical Anglicanism*, Jubilee Group, 1979.
19   *The Service of Humanity*, 1882: 37, quoted Orens op. cit.: 3.
20   In Leech and Williams, *Essays Catholic and Radical*, 1983.
21   op. cit. 21.
22   op. cit. 21-22.
23   *Theology,* January 1984: 66-68.
24   The claims of what he calls 'radical catholicism' have also recently been advanced by Stephen Platten, 'The attractiveness of radical catholicism', *Theology* November 1982: 429-37. While clearly within the liberal ethos, his ideas are markedly less

radical than some others: the social dimension is dismissed in three lines. See my comments in chapter 8.

25 David Martin, *A Sociology of English Religion*, Heinemann, 1967: 71ff. But a different view is taken by Alan Wilkinson, 'Requiem for Anglican catholicism', *Theology*, January 1978, who argues that the Catholic rejects the view of the Church of England as quintessentially English.

4 Ritualism and re-enchantment

1 Bryan Wilson, *Religion in Secular Society*, Watts, 1966: xiv.

2 Larry Shiner, 'The concept of secularization in empirical research', *Journal for the Scientific Study of Religion* 6, 1967: 207-20; reprinted in Kenneth Thompson and Jeremy Tunstall eds., *Sociological Perspectives*, Penguin, 1971.

3 David Martin *The Religious and the Secular*, Routledge and Kegan Paul, 1969; 15-17.

4 Gerth and Mills eds., *From Max Weber*, 1948: 139.

5 Shiner op. cit.: 468.

6 Peter L. Berger, *The Social Reality of Religion*, Faber, 1969: Chapter 5. This is the source for the following discussion.

7 Max Weber, *The Protestant Ethic and the Spirit of Capitalism*, Unwin, 1930: 182.

8 Michael Hill, *The Religious Order*, Heinemann, 1974: 247.

9 See David Martin's various writings on this topic, especially *Sociology of English Religion*, Heinemann, 1967.

10 Roy Wallis, *The Elementary Forms of the New Religious Life*, Routledge and Kegan Paul, 1984; see also Phillip E. Hammond ed., *The Sacred in a Secular Age*, University of California Press, 1985, especially the article by James T. Richardson.

11 But cf. Meredith B. McGuire, *Pentecostal Catholics; power, charisma and order in a religious movement*, Temple University Press, 1982.

12 Robert Bocock, *Ritual in Industrial Society*, Allen and Unwin, 1974: 68 treats Anglican Catholicism as 'an attempt to recover the sacred dimension in what was the most advanced nation, economically, politically and militarily at the time'. He refers to it as a major deviant case which reverses the general trend of desacralization analysed by Weber, in which a ritual religion is replaced by an ethical one, but he does not pursue the significance of this 'deviance' in any detail. Bryan Wilson (*Religion in Sociological Perspective*, Oxford University Press, 1982: 81) regards it as merely 'a passing and perhaps misplaced' reaction to long-term trends.

13 This account draws on Kenneth N. Ross, *Adoration of the Holy Sacrament*, All Saints Booklet No. 12, nd, (probably 1960s).

14 L. E. Ellsworth, *Charles Lowder and the Ritualist Movement*, Darton, Longman and Todd, 1982: 56 and 60.

15 S. F. Markham, *The Nineteen Hundreds*, 1951: 63. A similar mode of dealing with a turbulent ritualist was employed by Mervyn Stockwood when Bishop of Southwark in the case of Father Harris of Carshalton in 1959.

16 *The Catholic Faith in Practice*, 1918.

17 Conclusion of the 1906 Report.

18 Charles Smyth, *Cyril Foster Garbett*, 1959: 195.

19 Morse-Boycott op. cit. 1933: 250.

20 *Obedience: a Plea for Catholic Order*, 1929; *The Transactions of the Twenty-one*, 1930.

21 *Benediction in the Church of England*, published by 'The Voice from Worcester', 1934: 4.

22 Reg Groves, *Conrad Noel and the Thaxted Movement*, Merlin, 1967: 211.

23 Groves op. cit.: 220.

24 *Mirfield Essays in Christian Belief*, 1962: 263-64.

25 *Paths in Spirituality*, SCM, 1972.

26 Robert Bocock, *Ritual in Industrial Society*, 1974.

27 Robert Bocock 'Ritual: civic and religious', *British Journal of Sociology* 21, 1970: 285-97.

28 op. cit. 1970: 288.

29 Emile Durkheim, *Elementary Forms of the Religious Life*, 1912, especially Book III.

30 Norman Nicholson, contribution to Dewi Morgan, *They Became Christians*, Mowbray, 1966.

31 *Professional Ethics and Civic Morals* 1957.

32 Owen Chadwick, *The Victorian Church*, Vol. II, Black 1970: 310.

33 Michael Reynolds op. cit. 1965: 36.

34 Harold Ellis, *The Hand of the Lord*, Mirfield Publications, 1958: 48.

35 Colin Stephenson, *Merrily on High*, Darton, Longman and Todd, 1972.

36 Hugh McLeod, *Class and Religion in the Late Victorian City*, Croom Helm, 1974: 79-80.

37 Chadwick op. cit. 1970: 312.

38 Such as those by Mudie-Smith, Masterman and Booth.

39 op. cit. 1970: 317.

40 Bocock 1974: chapter 4.

41 Bryan Wilson, *Religion in Sociological Perspectives*, Oxford University Press, 1982: 81.

42 J. H. Shorthouse, *John Inglesant*, 1881 edition, Ch. 39.

43 H. Mol, *Identity and the Sacred*, Blackwell, 1976: 233.

44 Roger Lloyd, *The Church of England 1900-1965*, SCM, 1966: 287.

45 Paul. A. Welsby, *A History of the Church of England 1945-1980*, Oxford University Press, 1984: 240.

46 op. cit. 241.

47 'Noli me tangere: management skills of the parish priest' in David Martin ed., 'Crisis for Cranmer and King James', *PN Review* 13, 1979.

48   Alan Wilkinson, 'Requiem for Anglican catholicism', *Theology*,
     January 1978: 44-45.

5 Parishes and priests

General Bibliography
There is a vast number of books of variable quality about Anglo-
Catholic clergy and parishes, from parish hagiography to sober
academic tome. They all have their uses, in different ways, for a study
such as this. A selection is listed below.

A. T. Bassett, *St Barnabas, Oxford: a record of fifty years;* F. Bennett,
The Story of W. J. E. Bennett, Longmans, 1909; R. T. Brandreth, *Dr Lee
of Lambeth*, SPCK, 1951; Piers Brendon, *Hawker of Morwenstow,*
Cape, 1975; Kenneth Brill ed. *John Groser: East London Priest,*
Mowbray, 1971; A. J. Butler, *The Life and Letters of William John
Butler,* Macmillan, 1897; R. Bullivant, *Church of the Annunciation,*
Washington Street, Brighton, 1964; C. E. Byles, *The Life and Letters of
R. S. Hawker,* Lane, 1905; *The Church in Baldwin's Gardens,* J. T.
Hayes, 1875; O. Fielding Clarke, *Unfinished Conflict,* Citadel Press,
1970; J. Clayton, *Father Stanton of St Alban's Holborn,* Wells,
Gardner, Darton, 1913; J. Coombs, *Judgement on Hatcham,* Faith
Press, 1969; idem, *One Hundred Years on the Hill: St Peter's
Streatham, 1870-1970,* 1970; idem, *One Aim: Edward Stuart 1820-
1877,* 1975; F. L. Cross, *Darwell Stone,* Dacre Press, 1943; W. Crouch,
Bryan King and the Riots at St George's-in-the-East, Methuen, 1904;
Madge Darby, *The First Hundred Years at St Peter's London Docks,*
1966; S. Dark, *McKay of All Saints,* 1937; Nan Dearmer, *The Life of
Percy Dearmer,* Cape, 1940; G. A. Denison, *Notes of my Life,* 1878; B.
H. C. Dickinson, *Sabine-Baring Gould,* David and Charles, 1970; R. R.
Dolling, *Ten Years in a Portsmouth Slum,* Swan Sonnenschein, 1896;
Marcus Donovan, *After the Tractarians,* 1943; J. Embry, *The Catholic
Movement and the SSC,* Faith Press, 1931; L. E. Ellsworth, *Charles
Lowder and the Ritualist Movement,* Darton, Longman and Todd,
1982; G. A. ffrench-Beytagh, *Encountering Darkness,* Collins, 1973; T.
G. Fullerton, *Father Burn of Middlesborough,* 1927; S. Baring-Gould,
The Vicar of Morwenstow, Methuen, 10th edition, 1933; Reg Groves,
Conrad Noel and the Thaxted Movement, Merlin, 1967; R. H. Hadden,
An East End Chronicle, Hatchards, 1880; John Hester, *Soho is my
Parish,* Lutterworth, 1970; W. H. Hutchings ed. *Life and Letters of T. T.
Carter,* 1903; Kenneth Ingram, *Basil Jellicoe,* Centenary Press, 1936;
Br John Charles, *One Man's Journey,* Mowbray, 1972; J. O. Johnston,
Life and Letters of H. P. Liddon, 1905; W. Rowland Jones, *Diary of a
Misfit Priest,* Allen and Unwin, 1960; A. C. Kelway, *George Rundle
Prynne: a chapter in the early history of the Catholic Revival,*
Longmans, 1905; Ronald Knox, *A Spiritual Aeneid,* Burns Oates, new
edition, 1958; C. E. Lee, *Father Tooth: a biographical memoir,*
Truslove and Bray, 1931; Charles Lowder, *Twenty-one Years in St
Georges' Mission,* 1877; Lucy Menzies, *Father Wainwright: a record,*
Longmans, 1947; D. Morse-Boycott, *A Tapestry of Toil,* Faith Press,

1970; Nicholas Mosley, *The Life of Raymond Raynes*, Faith Press, 1961; Conrad Noel, *An Autobiography*, Dent, 1945; C. E. Osborne, *The Life of Father Dolling*, Arnold, 1903; Jack Putterill, *Thaxted Quest for Social Justice*, Precision Press, 1977; Maurice Reckitt, *P. E. T. Widdrington*, SPCK, 1961; idem ed. *For Christ and the People*, SPCK, 1968 (contains studies of the ideas of four Christian socialist clergy: Thomas Hancock, Stewart Headlam, Charles Marson and Conrad Noel); Michael Reynolds, *Martyr of Ritualism: Father Mackonochie of St Alban's Holborn*, Faber, 1965; G. W. E. Russell, *Arthur Stanton: a memoir*, Longmans, 1917; idem, *St Alban the Martyr: a history of fifty years*, George Allan, 1913; B. Scott-James, *Asking for Trouble*, Darton, Longman and Todd 1962; Colin Stephenson, *Merrily on High*, Darton, Longman and Todd 1972; idem, *Walsingham Way*, Darton, Longman and Todd 1970; T. P. Stephens, *Father Adderley*, 1943; Eleanor Towle, *Alexander Herriot Mackonochie: a memoir*, Kegan Paul, 1882; idem, *John Mason Neale: a memoir*, 1906; Maria Trench, *Charles Lowder: a biography*, Kegan Paul, 1882; J. H. C. Twisaday, *Thirty years at All Saints' Notting Hill*, 1964; Emmie Varwell, *Throwleigh: the Story of a Dartmoor Village* 1938; F. Verinder, *Stewart Headlam*, 1926; Bernard Walke, *Twenty Years at St Hilary*, Methuen, 1937; Evelyn Waugh, *The Life of Ronald Knox*, 1959; A. F. Webling, *Something Beyond*, Cambridge University Press, 1931; W. A. Whitworth, *A History of All Saints Margaret Street*, nd; Hugh Ross Williamson, *The Walled Garden*, 1956; J. Williamson, *Father Joe*, Hodder Stoughton 1963; A. Wilson, *Thy Will be Done*, World's Work, 1961; M. V. Woodgate, *Father Benson: Founder of the Cowley Fathers,* 1953; Edwyn Young, *No fun like work*, Mowbray, 1970.

Notes

1 R. C. K. Ensor, *England 1870-1914*, Oxford History of England Vol. XIV, Oxford University Press 1936; reprinted 1960.
2 Ensor op. cit. 140-41.
3 Wilson op. cit. 1966: 136-38.
4 J. Embry, *The Catholic Movement and the SSC*, Faith Press, 1931: 269-70.
5 Embry op. cit. 33-34.
6 Owen Chadwick op. cit. 1970: 337-38.
7 Ronald C. D. Jasper, *George Bell, Bishop of Chichester*, Oxford University Press, 1967, chapter 9.
8 Morse-Boycott op. cit. 271-73.
9 See *Church Times*, July-December 1959, and *Catholic Standard for Anglicans*, December 1972: 4.
10 *Church Times*, 24 April and 18 May 1959 and 14 April 1960; *Catholic Standard for Anglicans*, February 1971: 6. A recent example has been the furore over the icon of the Black Madonna at Great Torrington in Devon, which led to the first sitting of the Court of Ecclesiastical Causes Reserved since its institution twenty-one years previously. See *The Times,* 19 December 1984

and 19 February 1985. In this case, which appears to have been based as much on interpersonal conflict as doctrinal objection, the Court eventually decided largely in favour of the innovations.

11 Scott-James op. cit. 1962: 56.

12 Rowland W. Jones, *Diary of a Misfit Priest*, Allen and Unwin, 1960: 53-54.

13 Colin Stephenson, *Merrily on High*, Darton, Longman and Todd, 1972: 30.

14 Stephenson op. cit. 27.

15 Reg Groves, *Conrad Noel and the Thaxted Movement*, Merlin 1967: 231.

16 Stephenson op. cit. 77.

17 Davies op. cit. 1983.

18 Geoffrey Faber, *Oxford Apostles*, 1933; Penguin edition 1954: 211-26.

19 E. R. Norman, *Anti-Catholicism in Victorian England*, Allen and Unwin, 1968: 108ff.

20 Owen Chadwick: *The Founding of Cuddesdon*, Oxford University Press, 1954: 92; G. W. E. Russell, *Edward King, Sixtieth Bishop of Lincoln*, 1912: 34. The case against believing King to be homosexual is put by John A. Newton, *Search for a Saint: Edward King*, Epworth, 1977: 45ff.

21 Rayner Heppenstall, *The Intellectual Part*, 1963: 147 T. S. Matthews, *Great Tom*, 1974: 117.

22 Harry Williams: *Some Day I'll Find You*, Mitchell Beazley, 1982: 120-21.

23 Cf. McLeod op. cit. 113-14.

24 Horace Keast, 'A catholic notebook–VII', *Fiery Cross*, July 1943.

25 As shown by e.g. letter in *Catholic Standard for Anglicans*, January 1967: 5, and reaction to some of Colin Stephenson's writings.

26 Michael Daniel, 'The association between churchmanship and the Anglican clergyman's self-image', *International Conference of Religious Sociology* 1967; 'Catholic, Evangelical and Liberal in the Anglican priesthood', in David Martin ed., *A Sociological Yearbook of Religion in Britain* 2, SCM, 1968.

27 On the loneliness of the clergy, see Leslie Paul, *The Deployment and Payment of the clergy*, Church Information Office, 1964, chapter 5; cf Paul A. Welsby, *A History of the Church of England*, Oxford University Press, 1984: 131ff., and John Tiller, *A strategy for the church's ministry*, Church Information Office, 1983.

28 Daniel op. cit.; Cf Robert Towler, 'Puritan and Antipuritan: types of vocation to the ordained ministry', *A Sociological Yearbook of Religion in Britain 2*, SCM, 1969; Towler and Coxon, *The Fate of the Anglican clergy*, Macmillan, 1979.

29 Bryan Wilson op. cit. 1966; 136-38; Eric Carlton, 'The predicament of the Baptist minister', *New Society*, 7 January 1965: 11.

30 The early 1980s have seen a steady trickle of such conversions,

however, including some figures well-known in the Catholic movement. Proposals for the ordination of women seem to have been a major cause, also the vigorous restatement of a relatively mild liberalism by Bishop David Jenkins. The certainty of Roman authority will probably remain an attraction to Anglican Catholics, even if only a few take the major step of conversion.

6 The Religious orders

1 J. R. H. Moorman, *St. Francis of Assisi*, 1963: 42; quoted S. Campbell-Jones, *In Habit: an anthropological study of working nuns*, 1979: 210.

2 Graham Davies, 'Squires in the East End?', *Theology*, July 1983: 251.

3 J. H. S. Kent, 'The Victorian Resistance: comments on religious life and culture 1840-80', *Victorian Studies* 12, 1968.

4 C. P. S. Clarke, *The Oxford Movement and After*, Mowbray, 1932: 249.

5 W. J. Sparrow Simpson, *The History of the Anglo-Catholic Revival from 1845*, Allen and Unwin, 1932: 230.

6 Michael Hill, *The Religious Order*, Heinemann, 1974, chapter 10.

7 Sparrow Simpson loc. cit.

8 S. L. Ollard, *The Anglo-Catholic Revival*, Mowbray, 1925: 80-81.

9 For recent studies of Father Ignatius see Arthur Calder-Marshall, *The Enthusiast*, Faber, 1962, and Peter F. Anson, *Building up the Waste Places*, Faith Press, 1973.

10 cf. Rosabeth Kanter, *Commitment and Community: communes and utopias in sociological perspective*, Harvard University Press, 1972; P. Abrams and A. McCullough, *Communes, Sociology and Society*, Cambridge University Press 1976.

11 Peter Anson, *The Call of the Cloister*, SPCK, 1964.

12 Peter Anson, *The Benedictines of Caldey*, Catholic Book Club, 1940; xxvi-xxvii.

13 Anson loc. cit.

14 Geoffrey Moorhouse, *Against All Reason*, Penguin, 1969: 57.

15 Lively accounts of this period are in the two works by Anson referred to above.

16 Robert Southey, *Sir Thomas More, or Colloquies on the Progress and Prospects of Society*, 1829, Vol. II: 318.

17 Anson 1940: xix.

18 Anson op. cit. xvi and xxi.

19 *Life and Letters of W. J. Butler* 1897: 152-53.

20 The following account is drawn from Thomas Jay Williams, *Priscilla Lydia Sellon*, SPCK, 1965.

21 Quoted in Harold Ellis, *The Hand of the Lord*, Mirfield, 1958: 70.

22 *The Founders of Clewer*: 27.

23 op. cit. 29.

24 Pusey House MSS quoted Clarke op. cit. 251.

25 See note 9.
26 Clarke op. cit. 259.
27 On Benson and the Cowley Fathers see B. D. Williams, *With Wings as Eagles*, Cowley, 1953; M. V. Woodgate, *Father Benson of Cowley*, 1953; *Letters of R. M. Benson*; M. Smith ed., *Benson of Cowley*, Oxford University Press, 1980.
28 Ollard op. cit. 89-90.
29 On Caldey see the writings of Peter F. Anson referred to above. He was a member of the community.
30 On the Anglican Franciscans see *inter alia* Luigi Josa, *St Francis of Assisi and the Third Order in the Anglo-Catholic Church*, 1903; A. Clifton Kelway ed. *A Franciscan Revival: the Story of the Society of the Divine Compassion*, Whitwell Press, 1908; Kathleen E. Burne ed., *The Life and Letters of Father Andrew SDC*, Mowbray, 1948; Father Denis, *Father Algy*, Hodder and Stoughton, 1964; John R. H. Moorman, *The Franciscans in England*, Mowbray, 1974; Barrie Williams, *The Franciscan Revival in the Anglican Communion*, Darton, Longman and Todd, 1982.
31 On Mirfield see G. L. Prestige, *Life of Charles Gore* 1935; C. S. Philips et al. *Walter Howard Frere, A memoir*, 1947; *CR Mirfield 1892-1952*, 1952; James Carpenter, *Gore: a study in Liberal Catholic thought*, Faith Press, 1960; *CR Mirfield*, 1960; Nicholas Mosley, *The Life of Raymond Raynes*, Faith Press, 1961; *Mirfield Essays in Christian Belief*, 1962; Harry Williams, *Some Day I'll Find You*, Mitchell Beazley, 1982.
32 Moorhouse op. cit. 58.
33 Harry Williams, op. cit. 1982 gives a personal account.
34 Geoffrey Curtis CR, *William of Glasshampton: Friar: Monk: Solitary 1862-1937*, SPCK, 1947.
35 Moorhouse op. cit. 60.
36 Moorhouse op. cit. 262.
37 Ollard op. cit. 80.
38 For example, Richard Holloway ed., *The Anglican Tradition*, Mowbray 1984; Michael Marshall, *The Anglican Church Today and Tomorrow*, Mowbray, 1984; Geoffrey Rowell, *The Vision Glorious: themes and personalities of the catholic revival in Anglicanism*, Oxford University Press, 1983; Paul A. Welsby, *A History of the Church of England 1945-1980*, Oxford University Press, 1984; books in the *Faith and the Future* series published by Blackwell in 1983; the *Oxford Prophets* series published by the Church Literature Association.

7 Walsingham

General bibliography

Some of the history of the shrine is recorded in the periodical *Our*

Lady's Mirror (later the *Walsingham Review*). See also the illustrated guide *The Shrine of Our Lady of Walsingham containing the Holy House, England's Nazareth*, various editions; Heather M. Beaumont, *Sir William Milner*, 1985; Claude Fisher, *Walsingham: a place of pilgrimage for all people*, Salutation Press, Walsingham, 1983; A & J Gurney, *Walsingham: a place of pilgrimage for 700 years*, Walsingham Estate, 1981; Donald Hole and Colin Stephenson, *England's Nazareth: a history of the holy shrine of Our Lady of Walsingham*, Faith Press, 1959; A. Hope Patten, *Mary's Shrine of the Holy House, Walsingham*, Cambridge, 1954; Peter Rollings, *Walsingham in Times Past*, Countryside Publications, 1981; Bruno Scott James, *Asking for Trouble*, Darton, Longman and Todd 1962; Colin Stephenson, *Walsingham Way*, Darton, Longman and Todd 1970; Colin Stephenson, *Merrily on High*, Darton, Longman and Todd 1972.

In this chapter I also draw on material from my 1967-68 survey, and on periodic fieldwork from 1965 to the present day.

Notes

1   I owe this term, and the ideas behind it, to David Martin, *The Breaking of the Image*, Blackwell, 1980; see especially chapter 3.
2   *Report of the Royal Commission on Ecclesiastical Discipline*, 1904.
3   Robert Bocock, *Ritual in Industrial Society*, Allen and Unwin, 1974: 88; cf. Horace Keast, *Our Lady in England*, Society of Mary, 1984.
4   Colin Stephenson, *Walsingham Way*, Darton, Longman and Todd, 1970: 112.
5   Loc. cit.
6   Op. cit. 1970: 113. It is worth noting that Bernard Walke achieved a similar transformation at St Hilary in the heart of Methodist Cornwall.
7   Stephenson op. cit. 1970: 131.
8   *Our Lady's Mirror*, Jan. 1926.
9   *Our Lady's Mirror*, Winter 1955.
10   Quoted Stephenson 1970: 235.
11   A view also taken by Colin Stephenson: private communication.
12   Claude Fisher, *Walsingham: a place of pilgrimage for all people*, Salutation Press, Walsingham, 1983: 65.
13   op. cit. 67-8.
14   op. cit. 70.
15   op. cit. 68.
16   op. cit. 70.
17   op. cit. 15.
18   Robert Bocock, *Ritual in Modern Society*: 87.
19   David Martin, *The Breaking of the Image*, Blackwell 1980: 53.
20   op. cit. 44.
21   op. cit. 51, following Victor Turner.

22 Peter Rollings, *Walsingham in Times Past*, Countryside Publications, nd: 41.
23 The frequent employment in Catholic literature of quotations from Eliot's *Four Quartets* is itself interesting as suggesting a 'secret text' of the Catholic movement. The place of Catholicism in Eliot's life and work is discussed in a number of studies. See, for example, Peter Ackroyd, *T. S. Eliot*, Sphere Books, 1985.
24 A respondent in my 1968 enquiry.
25 Paul Ferris, *The Church of England*, Penguin, 1962; 232.
26 Brother John Charles SSF, *One Man's Journey*, Mowbray, 1972.

8 Catholic socialism

General Bibliography

Historical discussions drawn on in this chapter include: James Bentley, *Ritualism and Politics in Victorian Britain*, Oxford University Press, 1978: Stanley G. Evans, *The Social Hope of the Christian Church*, Hodder and Stoughton, 1965; K. S. Inglis, *The Churches and the Working Classes in Victorian England*, 1963; Peter d'A Jones, *The Christian Socialist Revival 1877-1914*, Princeton University Press, 1968; Ken Leech, 'The Christian Left in Britain 1850-1950' in Rex Ambler and David Haslam eds., *Agenda for Prophets: towards a political theology for Britain*, Bowerdean Press, 1980; S. Mayor, *The Churches and the Labour Movement*, Independent Press, 1967; E. R. Norman, *Church and Society in England 1770-1970*, Clarendon Press, 1976; John Oliver, *The Church and the Social Order*, Mowbray, 1968; John Orens, *The Mass, the Masses, and the Music Hall: Stewart Headlam's radical Anglicanism*, Jubilee Group, 1979; idem, *Politics and the Kingdom: the legacy of the Anglican left*, Jubilee Group, 1981; idem, 'Priesthood and prophecy: the development of Anglo-Catholic socialism' in Kenneth Leech and Rowan Williams eds., *Essays Catholic and Radical*, Bowerdean Press, 1983.

A sociological commentary is Robert J. Bocock, 'Anglo-Catholic socialism: a study of a protest movement within a church', *Social Compass* 20, 1973: 31-48.

Notes

1 See, for example, the attitude of the Catholic League to the Spanish Civil War, as recorded in Brian Doolan: *The First Fifty Years*, Catholic League, 1966.
2 E. R. Wickham, *Church and People in an Industrial City*, 1957; K. S. Inglis, *Churches and the Working Classes in Victorian England*, 1963.
3 'The Rich and the Poor One in Christ', 1858.
4 'Priesthood and prophecy: the development of Anglo-Catholic socialism' in Leech and Williams, 1983. I have been greatly influenced by John Orens' writings, which I have found among the most interesting recent commentaries on Christian socialism.

5   Davies, 1983: 252.
6   Kenneth Leech, 'The Christian Left in Britain 1850-1950', in Rex Ambler and David Haslam ed., *Agenda for Prophets: towards a political theology for Britain*, Bowerdean Press, 1980: 62.
7   Quoted in A. R. Vidler, *F. D. Maurice and Company*, SCM, 1957: 97.
8   Maurice, *The Prayer Book*, 1966: 200.
9   Manifesto of the Communist Party, 1848, Ch. 3, Part 1a.
10 Reynolds, 1965; Ellsworth, 1982.
11 R. Kenyon, *The social service of the Catholic Revival,* quoted Evans 1965: 150.
12 Davies, 1983: 255-56.
13 As indeed it remains to this day. In Davies' words, (1983: 257) 'as the Church becomes institutionally more marginal to society, the temptation may grow for many priests to hang on to those older assumptions. There may even be a Thatcher-factor encouraging belief in nineteenth-century perceptions of leadership! Concepts of priesthood are entangled with ideas of social position, caught in socially determined interpretations of leadership, authority and prophecy. Priesthood, rather than being seen as an enabling sacrament, has been perceived in terms of authority and the authentication of action.'
14 *The Mass, the Masses and the Music Hall: Stewart Headlam's radical Anglicanism*, Jubilee Group, 1979. I draw heavily on this in the following paragraphs.
15 Orens, 1979: 9.
16 Quoted Orens, 1979: 10.
17 E. R. Norman op. cit. 1976: 180.
18 Orens op. cit. 1981: 8.
19 Scott Holland quoted Norman op. cit. 183. Cf the impact of Fr Patten at Walsingham.
20 Norman op. cit. 184.
21 Norman loc. cit.
22 *Modern Churchman*, 1932.
23 Peter d'A. Jones, *The Christian Socialist Revival, 1877-1914*, 1968: 183-86.
24 Leech 1980: 65.
25 Lewis Donaldson, 'Church and socialism face to face', *Church Socialist*, October 1913: 4.
26 Norman 1976: 248.
27 Maurice Reckitt, *P. E. T. Widdrington*, SPCK, 1961: 56.
28 E. R. Norman 1976: 249.
29 P. E. T. Widdrington, 'The return of "The Kingdom of God"', in *The Return of Christendom*.
30 David G. Peck (1943) quoted Reckitt 1961: 79-80.
31 D. L. Munby, *God and the Rich Society*, 1961: 158; quoted Leech 1980: 67.
32 Conrad Noel, *Autobiography:* 91.

33   *Catholic Crusader,* 16 January 1933: 3 quoted Leech 1980: 69.
34   Quoted Orens 1981: 16.
35   According to Reg Groves, 'Introduction' to *The Catholic Crusade 1918-1936,* Archive One 1970: 20.
36   Groves op. cit. 6.
37   Kenneth Leech, 'Spike's lib: the resurrection of the Catholic social conscience', *Church Times,* 26 December 1975.
38   Preface to Leech and Williams 1983.
39   Susan Young, 'Jubilee Groupers still on the move', *Church Times,* 4 January 1985.

9 Conclusions

1   See Anthony F. C. Wallace, 'Revitalization movements', *American Anthropologist* 58, 1956: 264-81; and *Religion: an anthropological view,* Random House, New York, 1966.
2   Bryan Wilson, *Religion in Secular Society,* Watts, 1966: 140.
3   'Requiem for Anglican Catholicism', *Theology,* January 1978: 40-45.
4   Robert Towler, *Homo Religiosus,* Constable, 1974, Chapter 8.
5   John MacMurray, *Ye are My Friends,* Quaker Home Service Committee, 1979: 5.
6   Sara Maitland, 'A deaf movement?' in *Can These Dry Bones Live? Critical reflections on Catholic Renewal in the Church of England 1978-1983,* Jubilee Group, 1983.
7   Tom Hurcombe, 'What are the hidden agendas?' loc. cit.
8   W. S. F. Pickering, 'Religion—a leisure-time pursuit?' in D. Martin ed., *Sociological Yearbook of Religion in Britain,* 1, 1968.